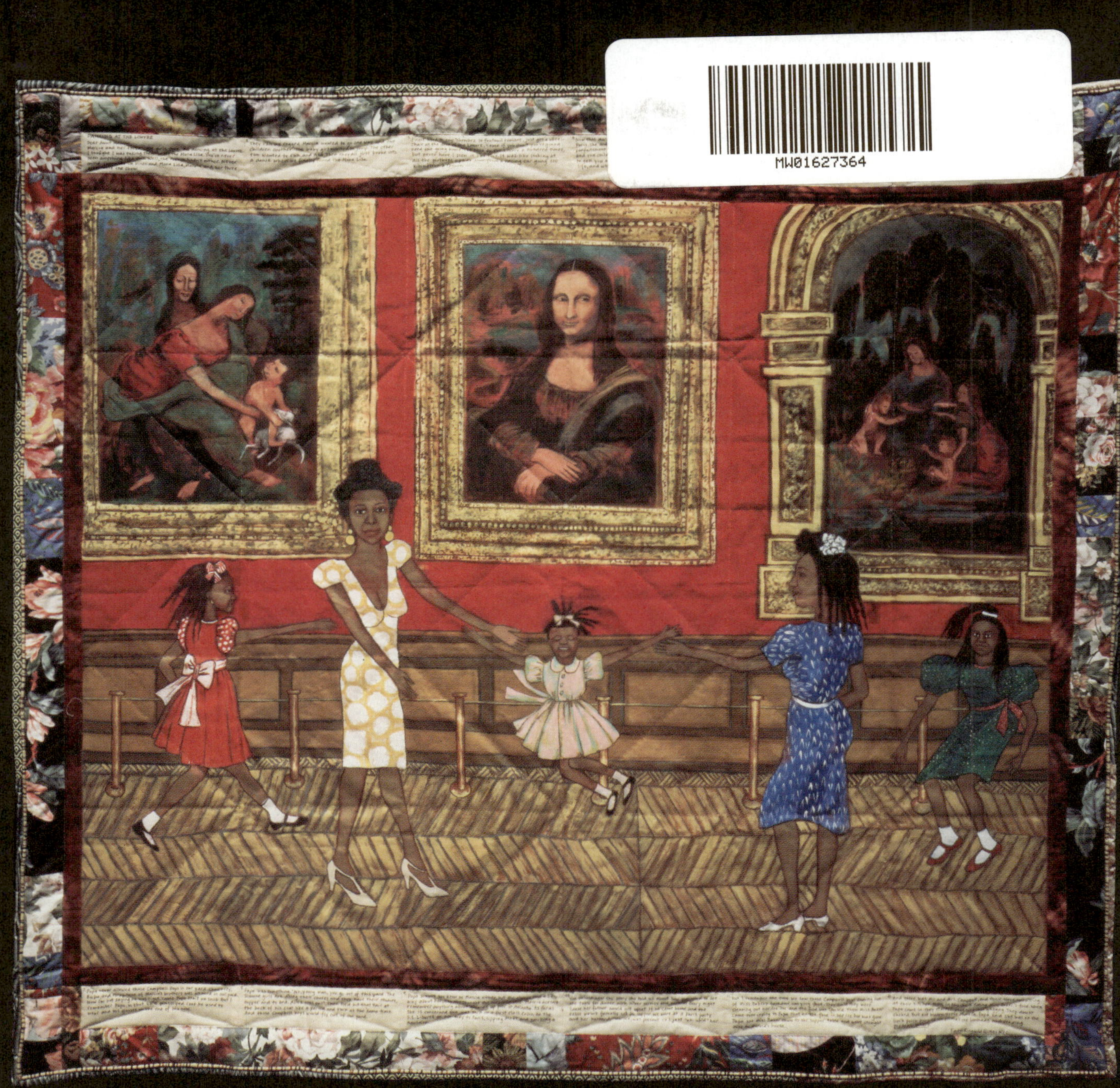

FAITH RINGGOLD

A View From the Studio

Curlee Raven Holton *with* Faith Ringgold

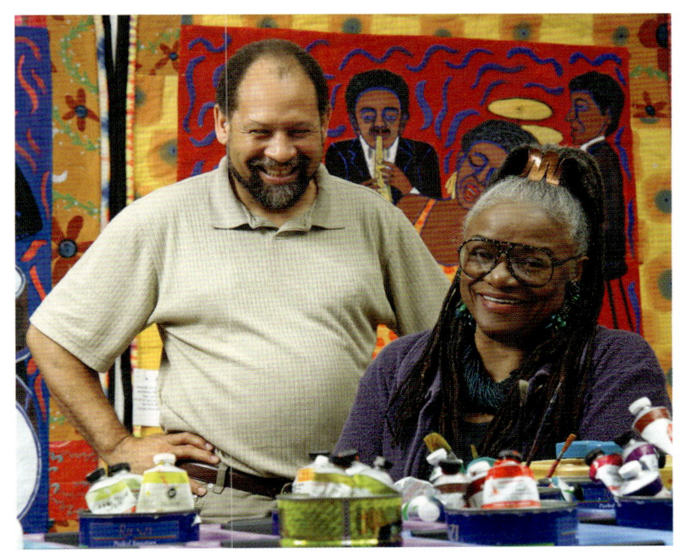

BUNKER HILL PUBLISHING
BOSTON

in association with ALLENTOWN ART MUSEUM

To Glee, my wife, and Ananda, my daughter

CRH

www.bunkerhillpublishing.com

First published in 2004 by Bunker Hill Publishing Inc.
26 Adams Street, Charlestown, MA 02129 USA

10 9 8 7 6 5 4 3 2 1

Library of Congress Control Number: 2004115985

ISBN 1 59373 045 4

Designed by Louise Millar

Printed in China

Foreword

Faith Ringgold is a modern master. Her deceptively simple compositions have a graphic strength and a directness that are the unmistakable product of a powerful artist. She has made unique contributions to the history of art, most notably in creating her signature story quilts. These works synthesize painting, quilting, and storytelling, bringing together the traditions of Western art with African American craft and folklore. Ringgold is a truth teller, whose honesty is evident in both her visual and verbal communications. Her paintings, sculpture, prints, and illustrated books have universal appeal, and I have enjoyed reading *Tar Beach* over and over at the request of my three-year-old son Noble.

Curlee Raven Holton has done an outstanding job of bringing this project to fruition. Under Curlee's leadership, an initially modest exhibition has grown into a larger one and is accompanied by this book and an original print. Holton is an excellent painter and printmaker in his own right, but has devoted himself to making this a success for one of his mentors, Faith Ringgold. The result is an intensely personal view of the artist from the studio, both hers in New Jersey and his at the Experimental Printmaking Institute (EPI). In the end, this book is the result of their years of collaboration.

In addition to having the privilege to publish this book, the Allentown Art Museum is delighted to publish an original print, designed by Faith Ringgold and pulled at EPI, *Mama Can Sing You Put the Devil in Me*. By underwriting the costs of this print, the Museum has proudly added to Ringgold's body of work. At the same time, the print has been sold to underwrite the costs of the project, made Ringgold's work available to a broader audience, and helped to promote the exhibition. The first print in the edition was generously donated to the Museum by our patrons Arnold and Deanne Kaplan.

This is Allentown's third book with Bunker Hill Publishing, and we are pleased to work with them to produce lively volumes of general interest that expand knowledge of our collections and special exhibitions. It is also my second project with Amy Pastan, the book's editor, with whom I published a book about Charles Willson Peale when she was acquisitions editor at the Smithsonian Institution Press. She has done an excellent job of maintaining the personal voice of the author.

The Museum is grateful to all who have purchased *Mama Can Sing You Put the Devil in Me* and to the County of Lehigh, Pennsylvania, for its support of this project.

David R. Brigham
The Priscilla Payne Hurd Executive Director
Allentown Art Museum

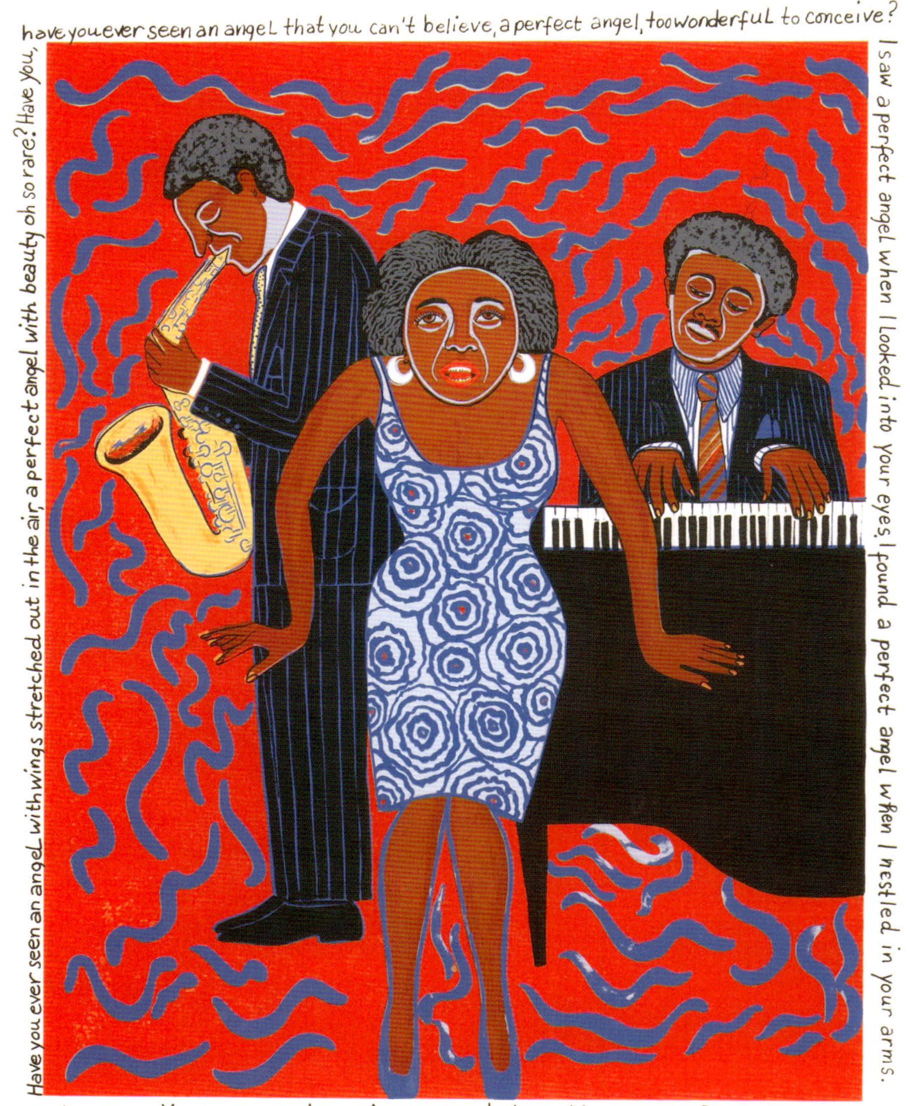

1 Mama Can Sing You Put the Devil in Me: Jazz Series, *July 28, 2004, serigraph, 22 x 30 in.*

Preface

During the past year, I met with David Brigham, executive director of the Allentown Art Museum, and Christine Oaklander, director of collections and exhibitions, to discuss the possibility of organizing an exhibition of work by a contemporary African American master artist. I presented them with a number of recommendations, including, of course, Faith Ringgold, for whom I'd been making prints since 1993.

David decided that Faith would be a terrific artist to feature, if it could be arranged. He had met Faith some years before, when he was a curator at the Worcester Art Museum. The museum purchased one of Faith's quilts, and David was impressed by the crowd of people who came to see Faith during her visit to Worcester. The staff of the Allentown Art Museum was equally aware of Faith's popularity, especially with children and teachers.

So, on one of my subsequent visits to Faith's studio, I gingerly asked if she would be interested in the possibility of an exhibition at the Allentown Art Museum. After a few moments of painful silence, she agreed. I quickly recommended that we consider curating the exhibit from her studio collection and the new *Jazz Series*. For the next six months we were involved in a whirlwind of activity. There were discussions about which works might be best in the show and what timetable would best fit into her complex exhibition schedule. She was concerned about giving this priority attention, given all the other projects that she had going on. I promised her that I would keep it simple, and that I would not be too demanding of her time in the planning of the exhibition. Characteristically, Faith simply raised her eyebrows at my protestations and responded with one of her thoughtful long "Ohs." She remained cautiously optimistic that I could deliver on my promise, but from time to time would throw up her hands in dismay. She would offer more than one mini lecture on why exhibitions were so much trouble, and acknowledged her own impatience with the myriad details required. She frequently says she prefers to have her gallery handle all of the arrangements when it comes to museum shows, but in truth, to some degree Faith oversees all her exhibitions. Somehow, we have survived the experience.

I have been privileged to see many of the works included in this book take shape in Faith's studio. Now, I invite readers and visitors to the exhibition to share in this exciting experience.

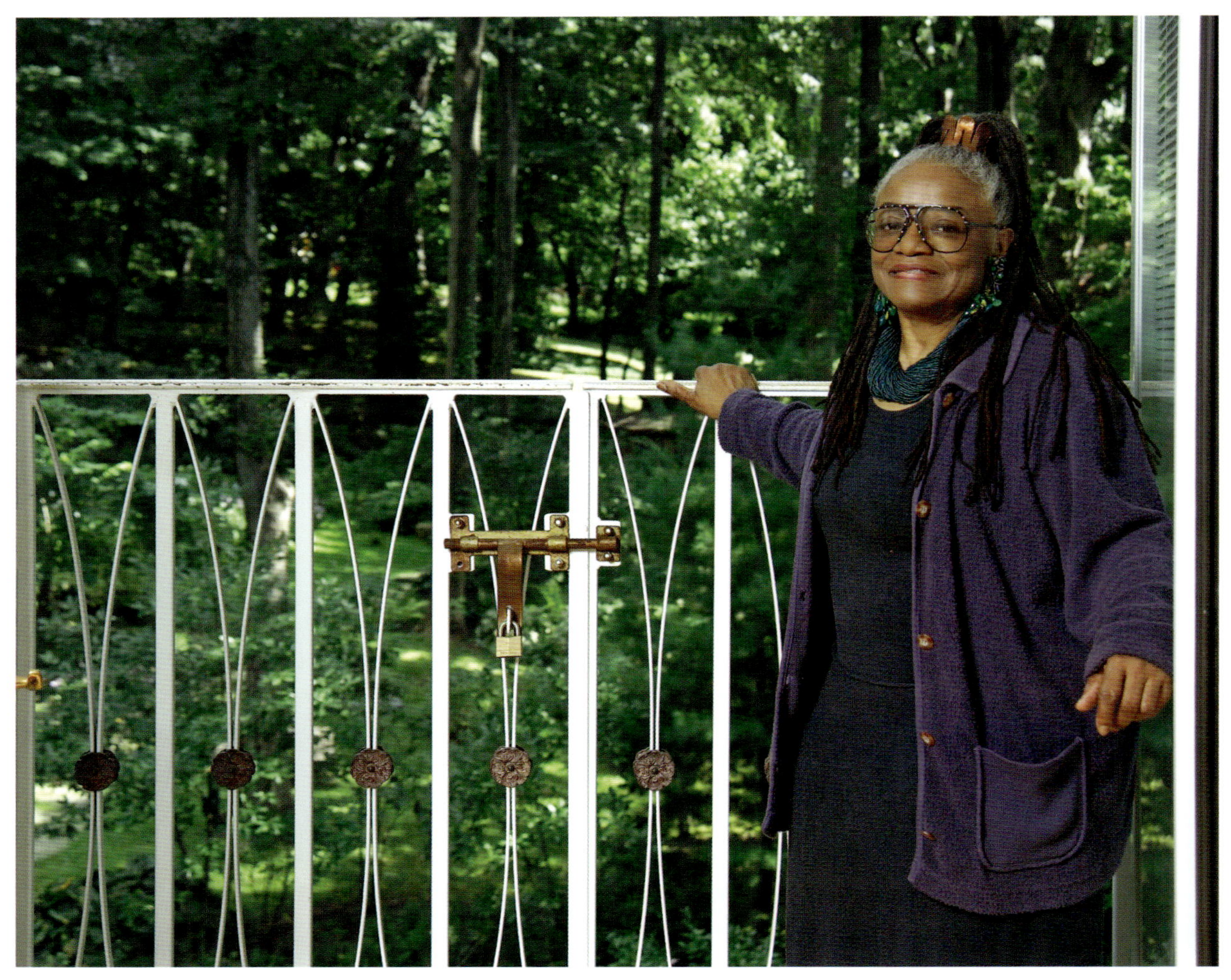

2 *Faith viewing garden at rear of studio.*

Faith Ringgold: A View from the Studio

During my life as an artist I have had the privilege and good fortune to find a number of mentors. This may not seem unusual, given that one of the oldest traditions in the practice of art is the apprenticeship of a young artist under the tutelage of a master. However, in the contemporary art world little of this tradition remains. There are many reasons for this, but the most apparent is that in a rapidly changing world there is no longer a lasting connection between artists of different generations. This makes my relationship with Faith Ringgold all the more significant. We have connected as artists, as collaborators, and perhaps, most significantly, she has become a mentor to me. I believe we are friends, but I accept the fact that as my mentor she will point me in directions I can't fully see on my own. The relationship is based on a mutual belief in the rich potential of the shared artistic experience and on our conviction that as artists we have something valuable to offer both to our own culture and to the broader art world as well.

I have known Faith personally for more than ten years, and for a large portion of that time, I have been the maker of her prints. I am certainly not the only one to consider myself one of her admirers. A few years ago I attended one of Faith's solo exhibitions at the ACA Galleries in the Chelsea section of New York City. After waiting for what seemed like an eternity, in a line that flowed out from the elevators to the main doors facing Twentieth Street, I finally was able to enter the building. I stood in line to catch the elevator and arrived on the fifth floor to face yet another line, snaking its way through the gallery to a table stacked with books. Behind the table Faith was dutifully signing each copy with a personal note.

I respectfully claimed a spot in the book signing line only because I wanted to get close enough to Faith to whisper a business detail in her ear, and it seemed inappropriate to bypass the line of people who had waited patiently to see her. Just when I was about to give up and slip away to the wine table, one admirer asked me if I had ever met Faith and explained that she "just loved her to death." I explained that I made some of Faith's prints, and the woman's face instantly lit up. She proudly told me that she tried to attend all of Faith's New York openings and underscored the point that she had all of Faith's books. She went on to say that I was so fortunate to know Faith, and that I was "truly blessed, truly blessed" to be able to work with her. She was right. I have been blessed in my relationship with Faith, a relationship based on a mutual appreciation of creative freedom and my profound respect for her accomplishments. Needless to say, I stayed in line lest the woman think I was disloyal!

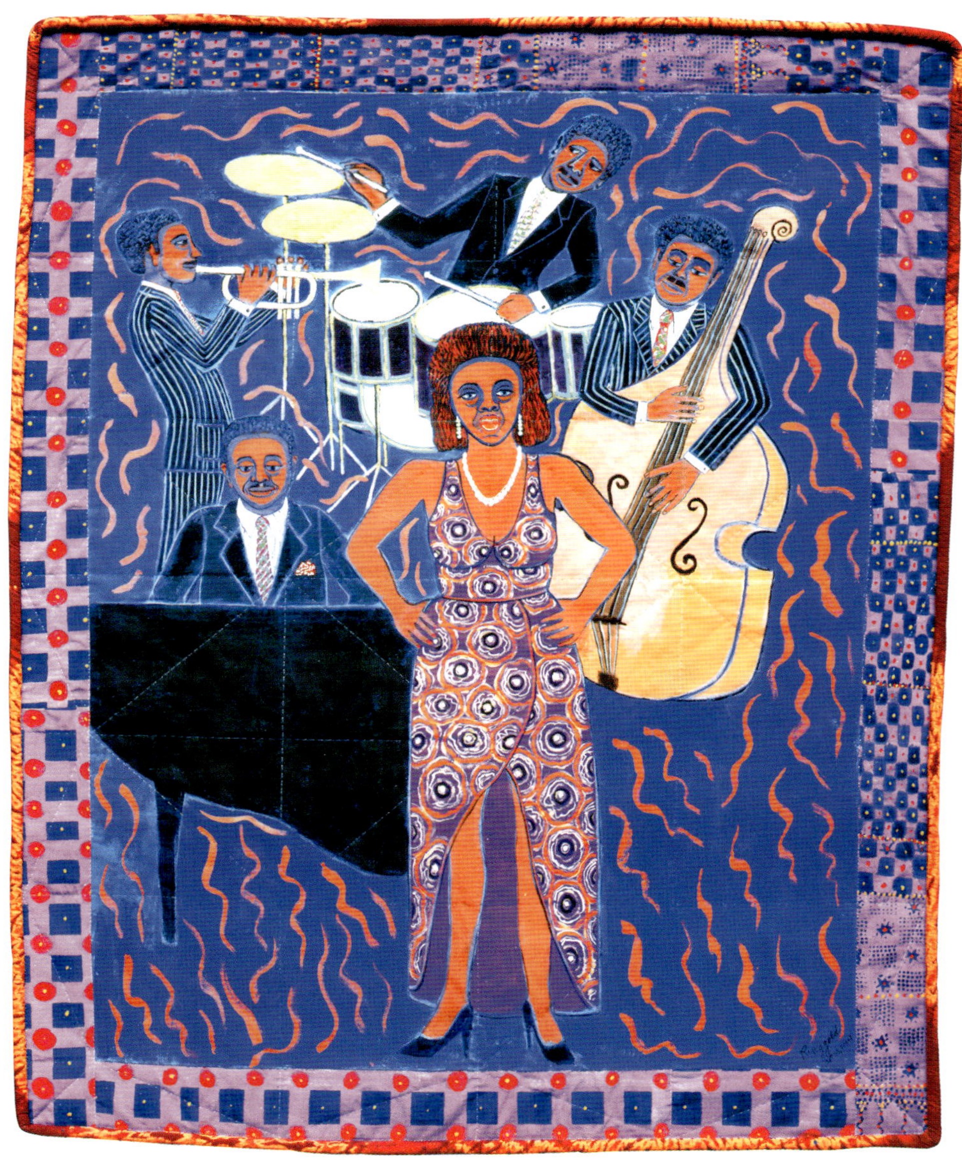

3 *Come On Dance With Me, Jazz Quilt # 2, acrylic on canvas, fabric, 82 1/2 x 67 in, 2004*

Art without Barriers

"... I wanted to make a difference ... I decided I was going to use art to do it."

I have lectured frequently on Faith's career as an artist and the important role she plays in the establishment of the contemporary African American artistic canon. She is unquestionably one of America's most prominent living artists and has created a body of work that spans almost fifty years. Her work not only documents the African American experience and has complex layers of social commentary, it also represents her interest in the dynamics of color and issues of composition and form.

In my experience, the work of an artist is always closely aligned with the life of the artist. In Faith's case, her work bears testimony to her fight to achieve acceptance and recognition in a world that is both racist and sexist. She is to the stuffy boundaries of the art world what a civil rights advocate is to injustice. She is an Earth Mother figure, nurturing everyone's children, as well as a daughter, carrying on a proud tradition of multiple accomplishments instilled in her by her own determined mother. The Faith I have come to know is subtle and subversive in her art-making. Her messages can shout or be subliminal at her choosing. She has been called a feminist, but she is quick to remind us that the feminist movement did not naturally seek out faces that looked like hers. Rather she, with the force of her presence, pushed the movement and claimed inclusion. She is angry, and yet she is not consumed by anger. On one plane, Faith is a figurative artist, whose paintings are sequels to and iterations of a much larger story; yet, she is also a metaphorical artist, whose amazing intellect is evident in the portrayal of her figures.

Faith's story is complex. Her talents as a young artist were the pride of her family, but not so obvious to all her teachers. She often tells the story of her first attempt to render a mountain scene. In a critique of her efforts, one of her teachers told her emphatically that she could not draw. A less secure student might have been scarred by such a remark, but for Faith, this was simply a challenge—a challenge she could easily accept. Being a New Yorker defined Faith's world view. In her urban landscape, the only mountaintops were the tar-covered rooftops of New York City hi-rises. Ringgold's quiet response to her teacher was, "Oh, yes. . I can draw." It was to be the first public announcement of her decision to become an artist regardless of the barriers.

To truly understand Faith's work, one has to consider the major influences that shaped her life and influenced her career: the legacy of slavery, the vibrancy of the Harlem Renaissance, the impact of blues and later jazz, the painful experience of segregated schools, the seemingly impenetrable walls of the art world for people of color, the strong values instilled in her by her family, and Faith's own tenacity. However, I initially only saw Faith and her work through the limited eyes of what I read and saw in the few publications that presented black art and chronicled the rise of what would later be called "outsider art." Faith had established her voice early on in the black arts movement of the 1960s. Her work during that time revealed a distinct and powerful vision that spoke directly to her desire for personal and artistic freedom. She was outspoken in her attitude and in her work, and although these characteristics have remained prominent features of her style, the work has expanded to include different media—from paintings and prints to quilts to soft sculpture. Her venues have shifted from the visual arts to the literary arts, and her desire to live a creative existence has led her to embrace a lifestyle that resembles one of her canvases: committed to resolving issues of race, gender, and class; orchestrated, but with spontaneous splashes of color and whimsy.

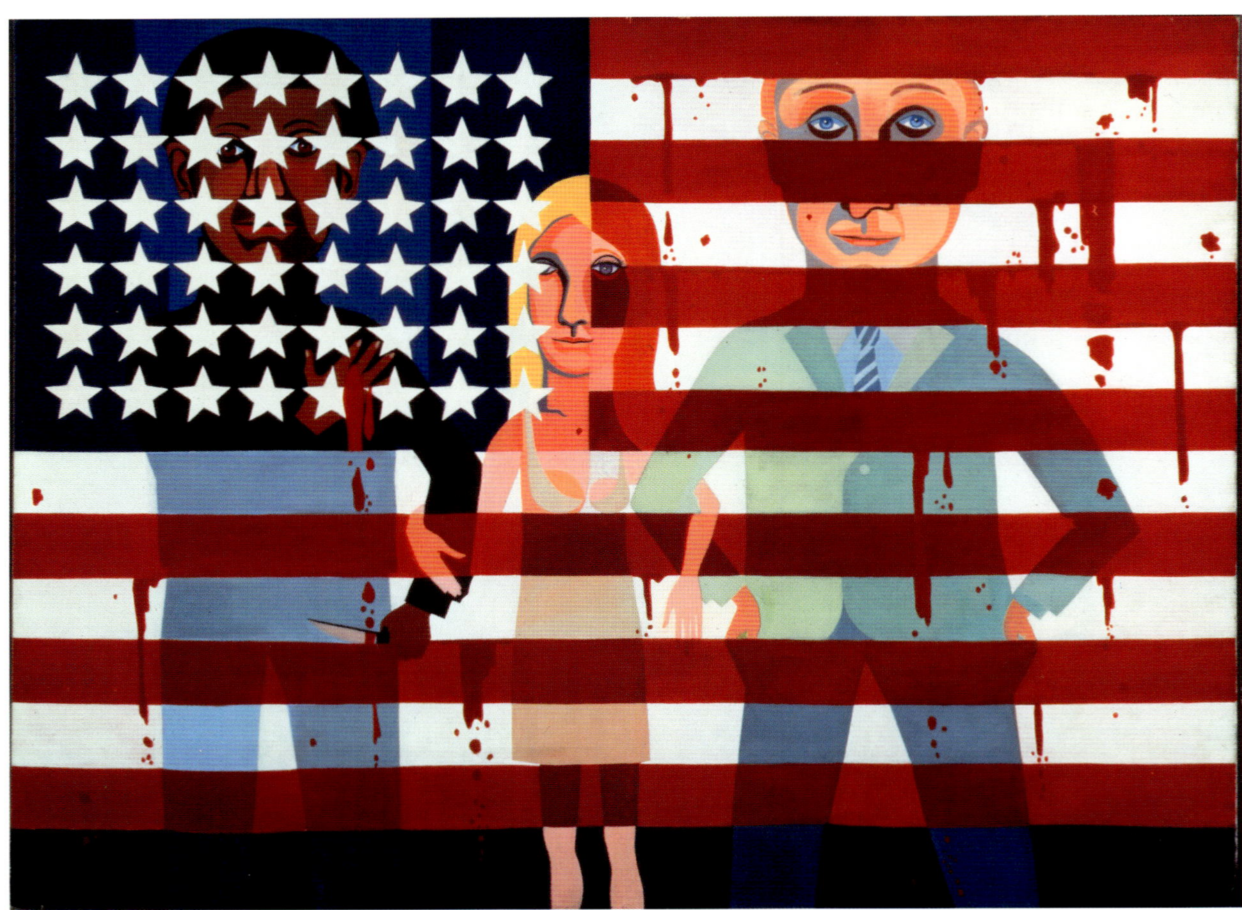

4 The Flag is Bleeding: The American People Series #18*, 1967, oil on canvas, 72 x 96 in.*

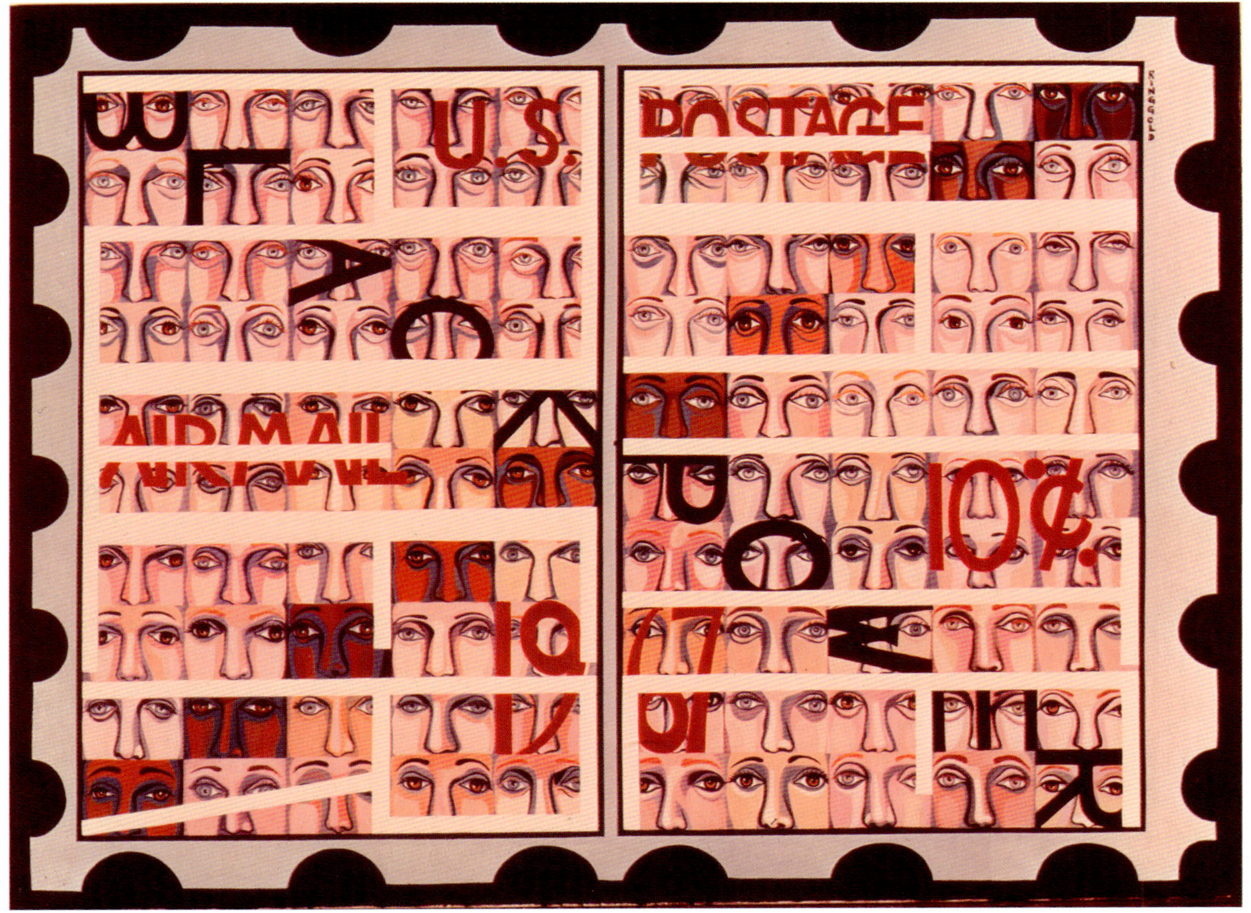

5 U.S. Postage Stamp Commemorating the Advent of Black Power: The American People Series #19*, 1967, oil on canvas, 72 x 96 in.*

It was during the 1960s that Faith wore an Afro and adopted the African garb that she still wears today. However, the Afro gave way to the corn row braids of the 1970s and then to dreadlocks in the 1980s. Faith's powerful works of that era, such as *The Flag is Bleeding*, from her *American People* Series, 1967, became emblematic of the times.

Two other seminal works of that period were *U.S. Postage Stamp Commemorating the Advent of Black Power*, from the same series, and the painting *Die*, from 1967. *Die* was the piece that resonated with me most as a young student because it was both powerful and

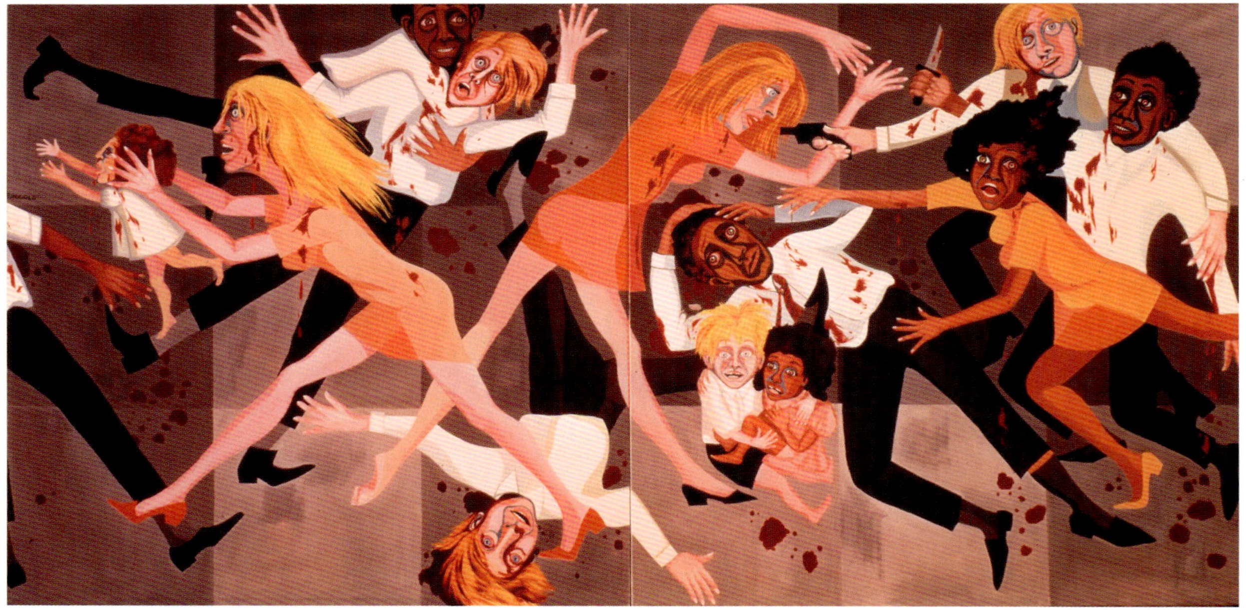

6 Die: The American People Series #20*, 1967, oil on canvas, 72 x 144 in.*

subtle. It also captured the conflicting emotions of many black Americans that as devoted citizens they had been betrayed by their country. As I developed my own artistic vision, Faith personified for me what it meant to be a black artist; her left hand was raised in the black power salute while her right hand held a paintbrush. She decided to use her work as a weapon in defense of her very existence as a black American, as a woman, and as an artist.

My first encounter with what some have referred to as the "Ringgold Experience" occurred in the spring of 1993, when I first visited her studio in New York City's Garment District at Thirty-eighth Street between Eighth and Ninth Avenues. Faith had been invited to Lafayette College, where I teach, as a Grossman Visiting Artist. As a part of that residency, she invited students and faculty to visit her New York studio prior to her first visit to the Lafayette campus. Lafayette College is considered one of the leading liberal arts colleges in the country. It is situated in the Lehigh Valley in Easton, Pennsylvania, and has an enrollment of approximately 2,200 students.

The students and I filed up the stairs, and the appointed leader knocked timidly on the studio door. Faith answered the door quickly and immediately took a step back. There were twenty Lafayette visitors squeezed tightly together on the tiny landing.

Before that first encounter, I had first seen some of Faith's work in Buffalo, New York, at the Albright-Knox Art Gallery. My wife and I were visiting from Cleveland, Ohio, where we lived at the time, and after wandering through the exhibition we walked into a

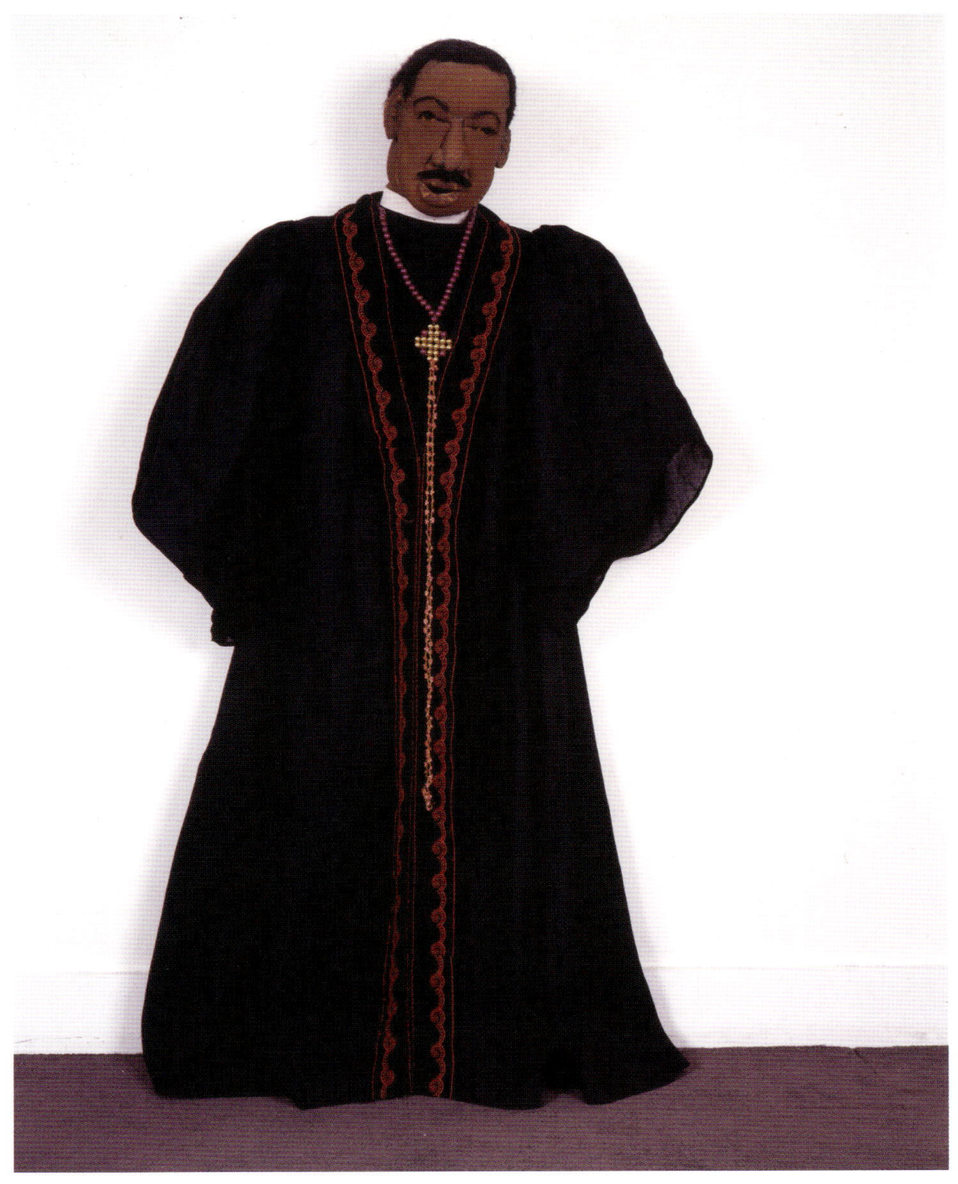

7 Martin Luther King, Jr: Portrait Mask Series, *1975, mixed media soft sculpture, life size.*

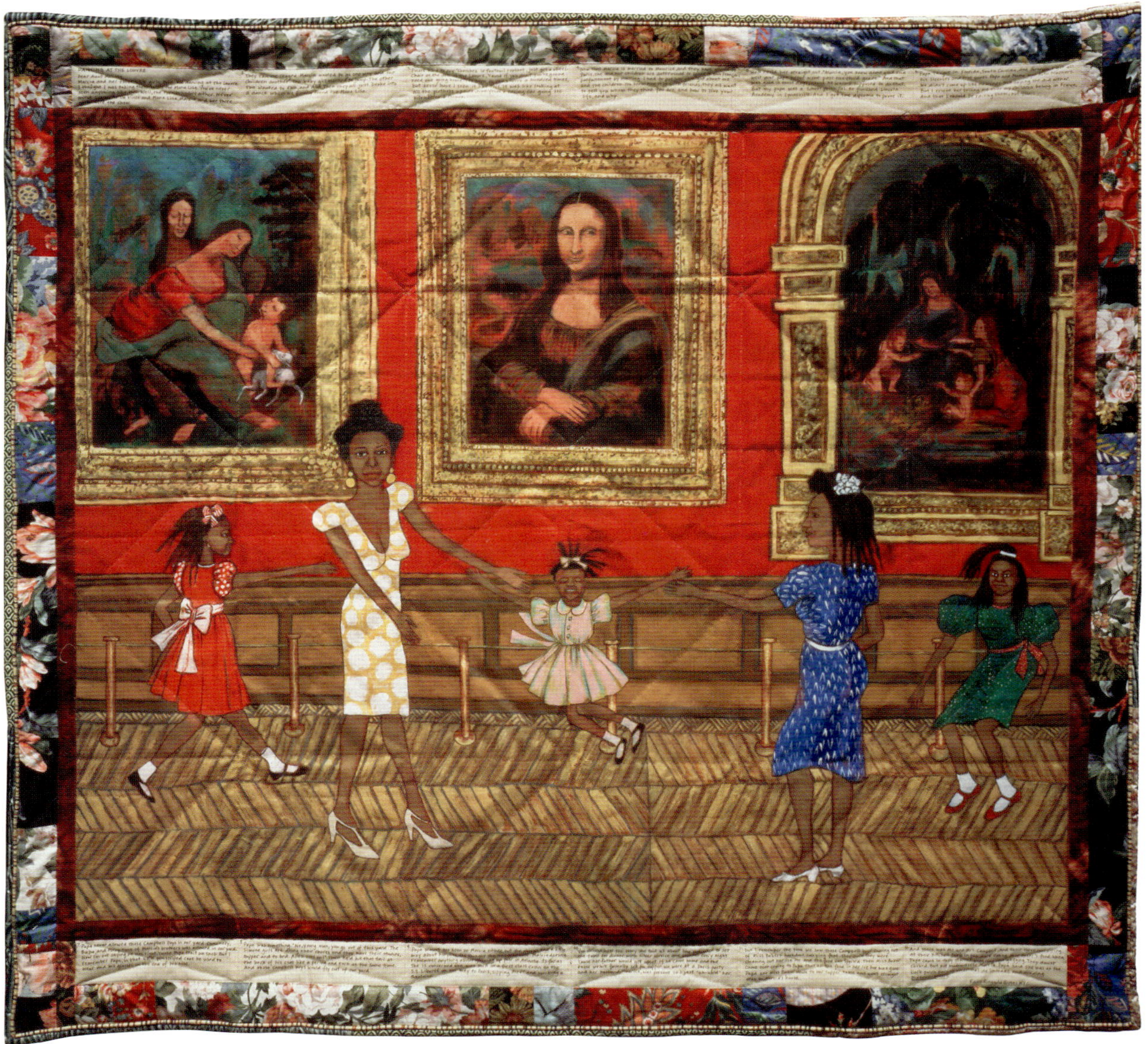

8 Dancing at the Louvre: The French Collection Part 1: #1, *1991, acrylic on canvas; printed, tie-dyed, and pieced fabric, 73 1/2 x 80 1/2 in.*

gallery that held an installation of Faith's pieces *Martin Luther King, Jr*, 1975, and *The Wake and Resurrection of the Bicentennial Negro*, of 1976. Images of black people in a traditional institutional exhibition space were a surprise to us and a visual delight, and we spent the afternoon enjoying her work. I was also aware of Faith's achievements as a writer due to her acclaimed *Tar Beach*, published in 1991. This award-winning children's book followed Faith's renowned *Tar Beach* quilt of 1988. I had seen *Tar Beach* at bookstores and had read magazine articles about Faith's popularity as a lecturer and storyteller among teachers and librarians. There was a period in my life when I read this book to my youngest daughter almost nightly, and her signed copy was kept out of reach from her perennially jelly-smeared fingers until she was able to whisk it away from her parents and place it on her own precious shelf of collectables.

I was delighted to come face to face with this legend, who gave us a wide smile and greeted each student warmly. She wore a long billowing African dress, and as she moved, her many bracelets jingled with their own rhythm. Her hair was arranged in dreadlocks and draped the sides of her face, framing her features very much like the regal bronze sculptures of Africa. She offered drinks and comfortable chairs. At first, the students, awed by her presence and their first studio visit, were uncharacteristically quiet, absorbing every moment of the experience, but soon there was a wonderful flow of conversation as Faith put everyone at ease.

From that first visit to her studio years ago, it was Faith's work that would remain etched in my memory.

There were three different works mounted directly onto the wall. Each canvas had been stapled along the edges, and after the application of paint, each began to shrink, stretching and pulling inward against the staples. Each canvas had a primary color applied as a background field, and clearly each was at a different stage of development. You could see the preliminary drawing still apparent to some degree on each painting, even though areas were painted in completely. Near the paintings were her carts, lined with rows of coffee cans full of different sized brushes and stocked with jars of bright acrylic paints. She pointed to the paintings one by one and explained how she worked on them simultaneously, moving from one to the other like a conductor of an orchestra.

As unfinished canvasses, the works on the wall had not yet been framed in Ringgold's signature borders, made of beautiful fabrics and embroidery. My students and I had the privilege of seeing newly conceived works that were still in the conceptual stage of development and would eventually join her *French Collection Series*. That series included earlier works, such as *Dancing at the Louvre: The French Collection Part I, #1*,1991 and *Picasso's Studio: The French Collection Part I, #7*, 1991.

Later works in the series would include: *Jo Baker's Birthday: The French Collection Part II, #9*, 1993. Faith's use of the narrative as a tool of liberation for her subjects is perhaps the most powerful aspect of her art. She uses her paintings to redeem the African American family and the black psyche from the alleyways of American history.

Dancing at the Louvre is the first quilt in the *French Collection Series*. It records the visit Willia Marie Simone and her friend Marcia made to the Louvre in Paris. The children dance across the floors of the galleries in view of famous masterpieces by Leonardo da Vinci–*Mona Lisa, The Virgin and Child with St Anne, The Virgin of the Rocks*. The children portrayed are Faith's grandchildren.

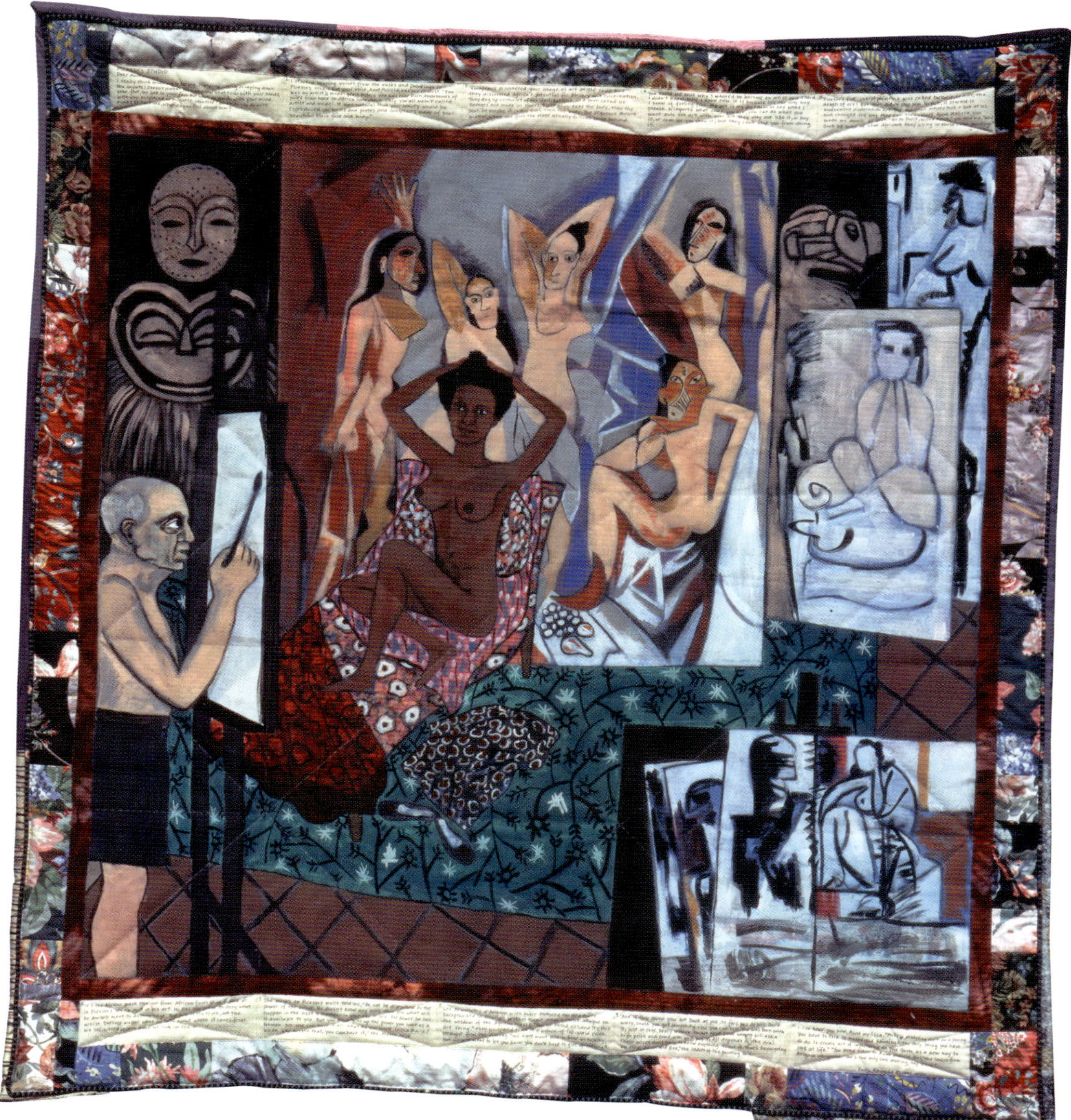

9 Picasso's Studio: The French Collection Part 1: *#7, 1991, acrylic on canvas; printed, tie-dyed, and pieced fabric, 73 x 68 in.*

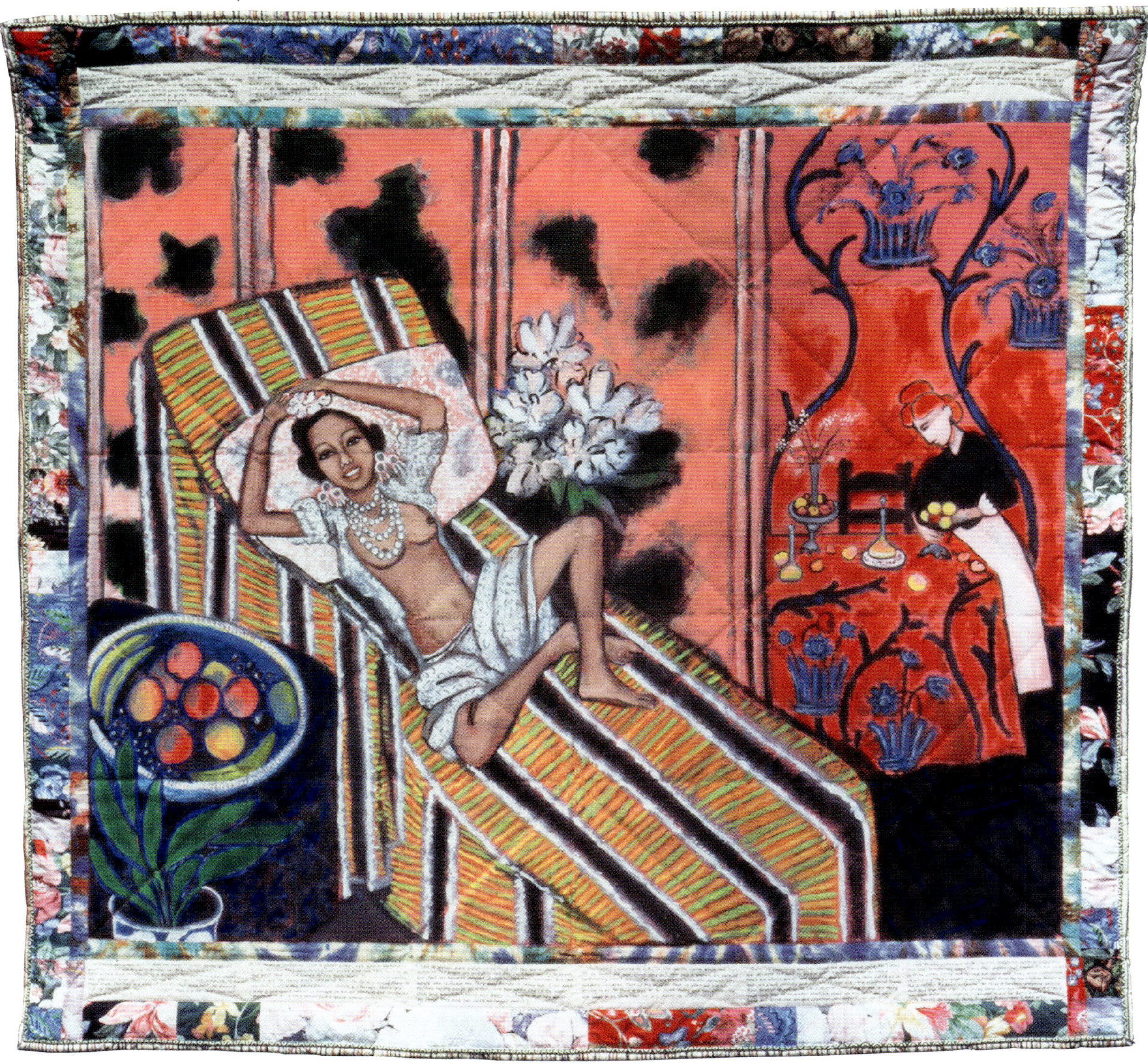

10 Jo Baker's Birthday: The French Collection Part II: #9, *1993, acrylic on canvas: printed, tie-dyed, and pieced fabric, 74 x 79 in.*

The series is very much about the freedom Faith felt as an artist working in Paris. It also continues her personal journey as a black woman, seeking freedom of movement and expression in one of the most sacred art institutions in Western civilization. She almost single-handedly removed the shackles placed on the possibilities for black people when she sent Willia Marie Simone off to dance at the Louvre.

Faith arrived at Lafayette on April 7, 1993. I know the exact date because the single word "Faith" is marked in big letters on my planner for that year. It was only my second year teaching at Lafayette, and I had just established the print program. The print studio had temporary space in what was formerly a small single-family dwelling on the college campus. We had a small Brand etching press, which at that time was located in the living room, and we processed the plates in what had been the kitchen sink.

I remember the excitement and anticipation that my students and I felt at having an artist of Faith's stature come into our small classroom. They showed her some of their prints and discussed art and politics. They listened to her with rapt attention as she told them about her disastrous first critique and learned that she had never seen a mountain as a child growing up in Harlem. Faith explained that, faced

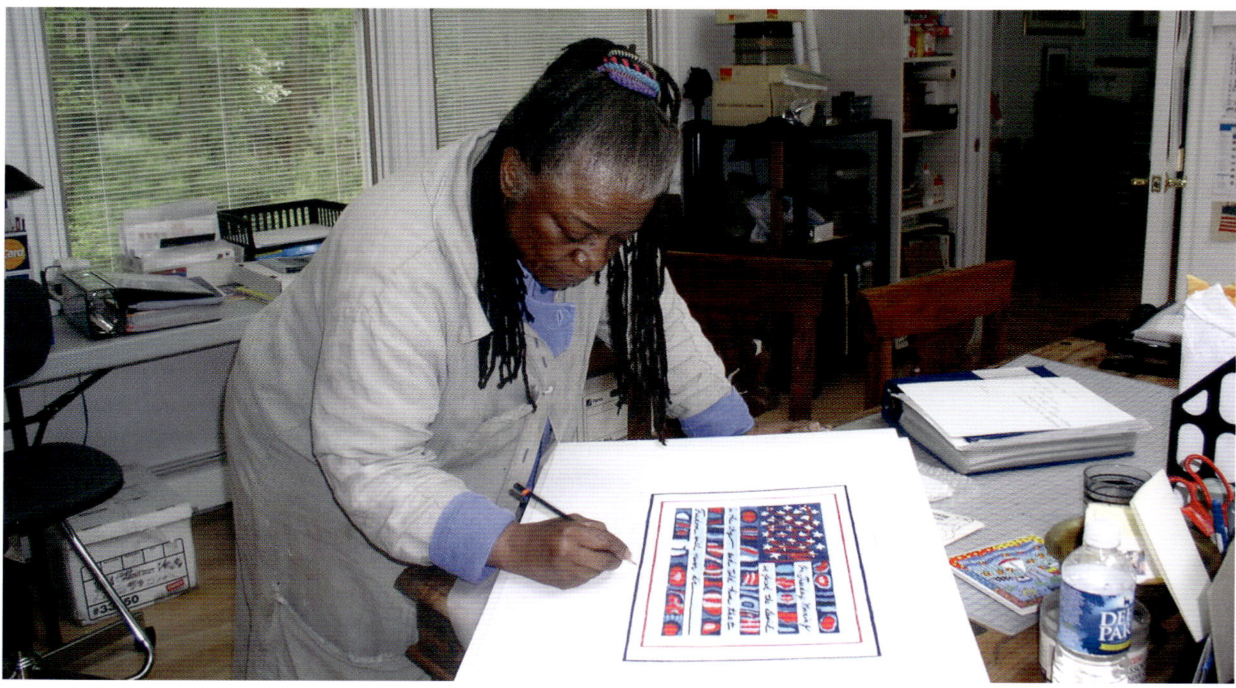

11 *Faith Ringgold signing* Freedom Flag Story #1, *May 30, 2003.*

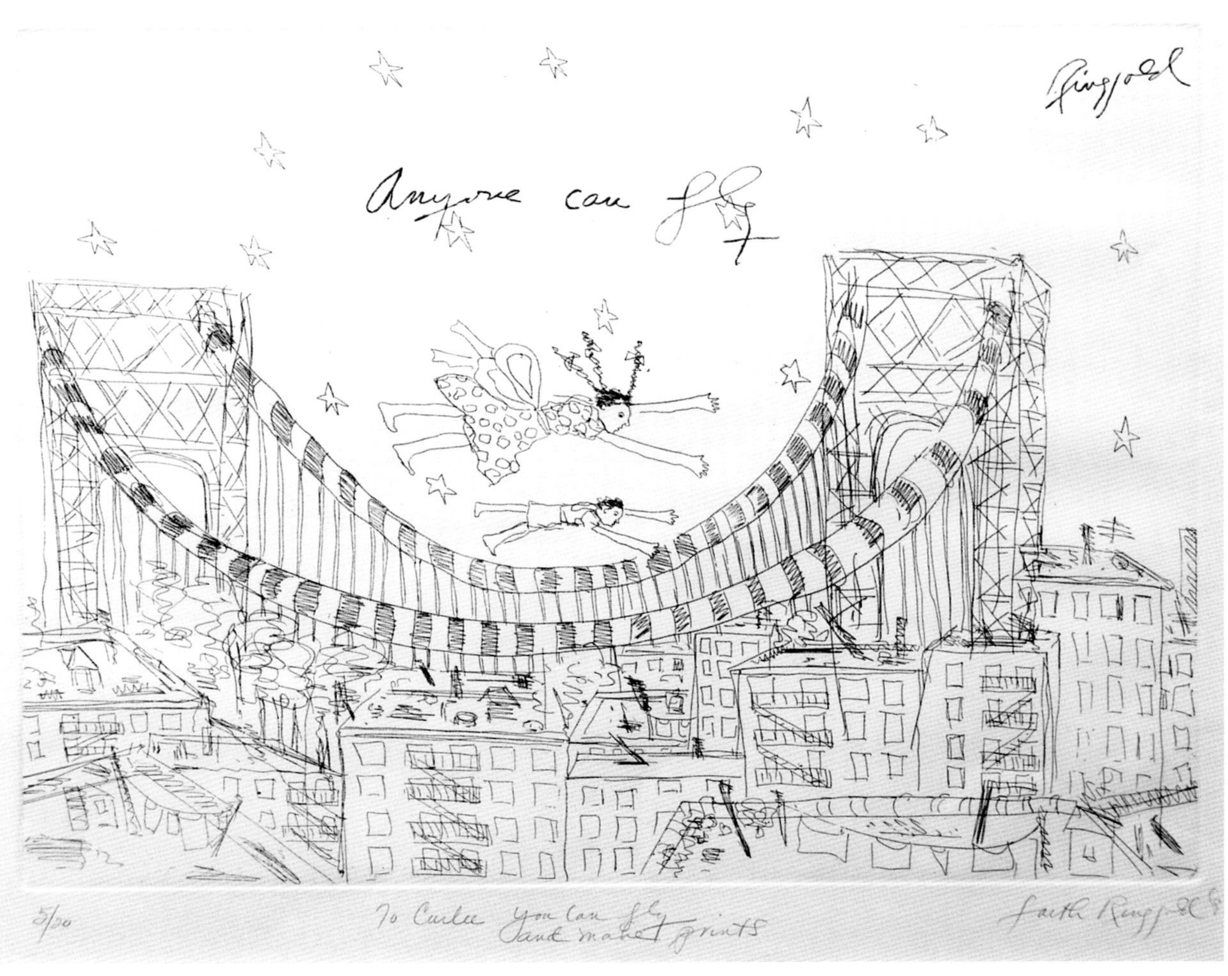

12 Anyone Can Fly, *etching proof plate 1993, printed 1997.*

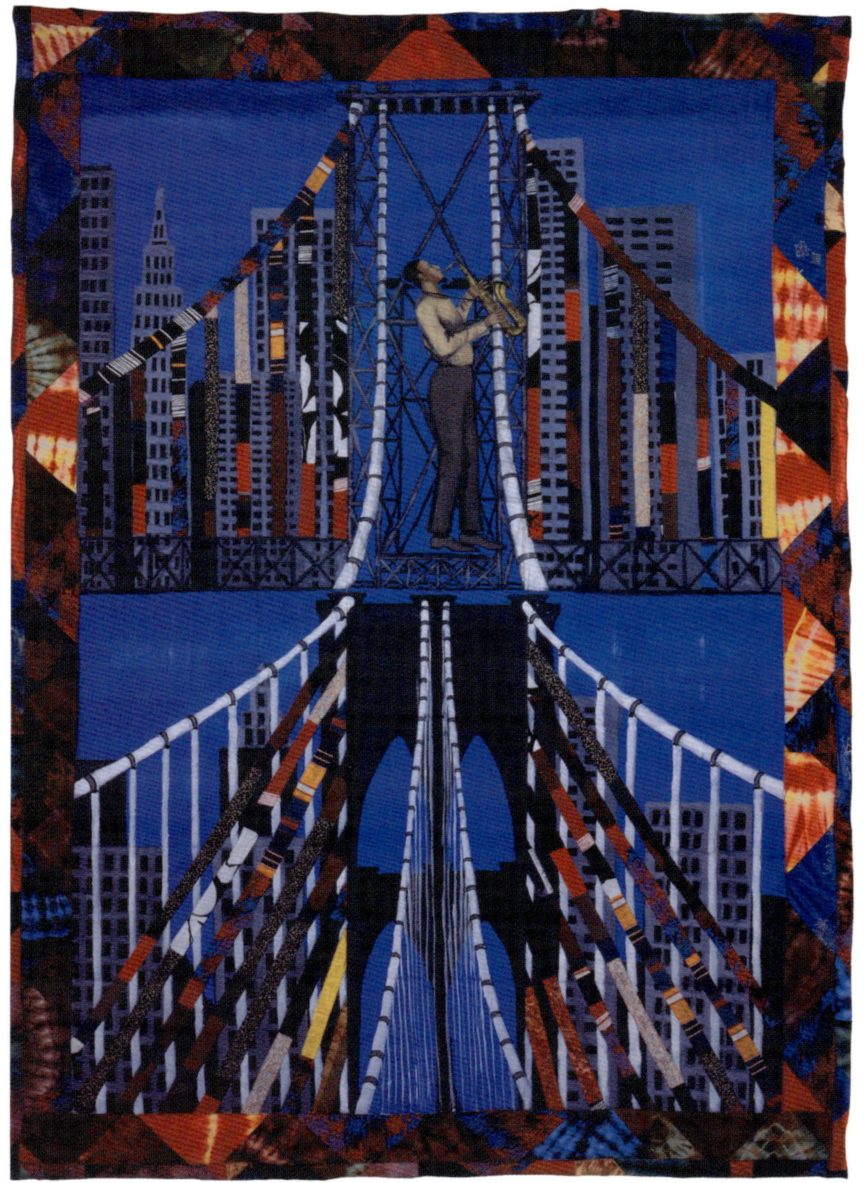

13 Sonny's Quilt, *1986, acrylic on canvas; appliquéd, printed, and pieced fabric, 84 1/2 x 60 in.*

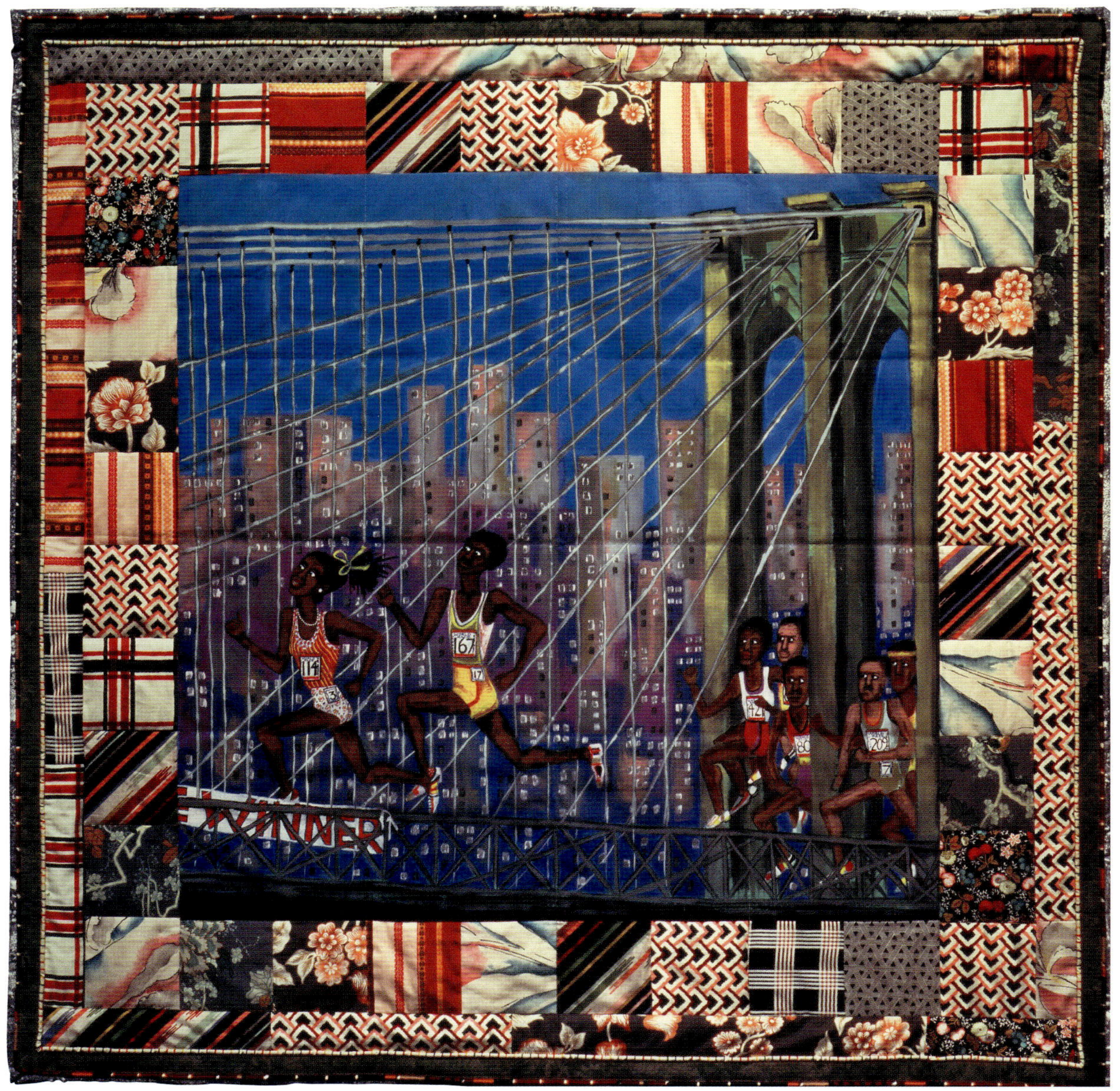

14 The Winner: The Woman on a Bridge Series #4, *1988, acrylic on canvas; printed, dyed, and pieced fabric, 68 x 68 in.*

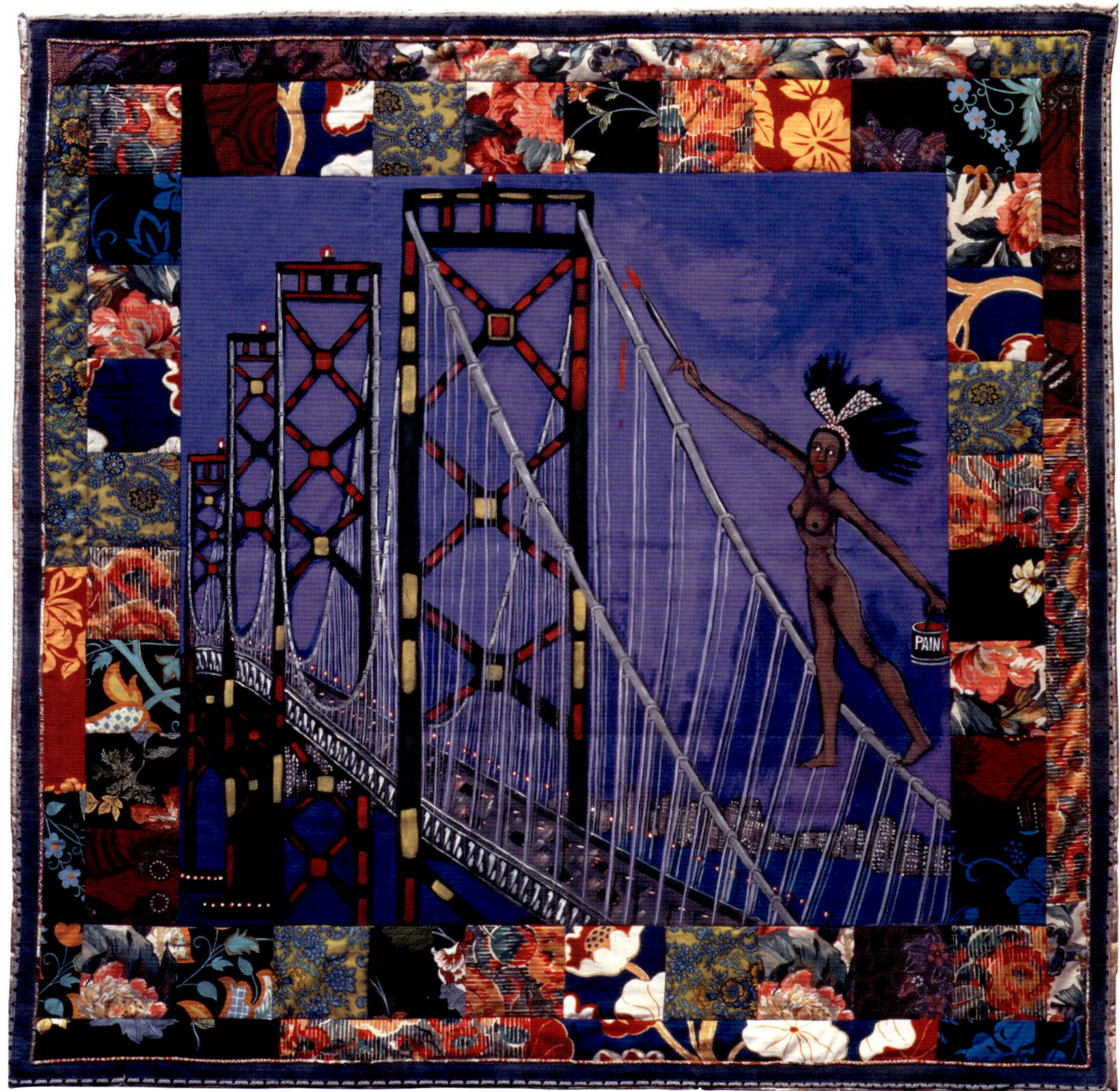

15 Woman Painting the Bay Bridge: The Woman on a Bridge Series #3, *1988, acrylic on canvas; printed, dyed, and pieced fabric, 68 x 68 in.*

with the assignment, she simply decided to draw what she imagined mountains would look like. She went on to tell my students more inspiring stories about her early years in Harlem and her struggles as a young artist, but she made the message universal: never give up on your dreams.

When the students ran out of questions, I invited Faith to sit at a table in the studio where I had previously prepared a plate, and I provided drawing tools for her. She seemed a little bit surprised, but after only a moment's hesitancy she sat right down and began to draw. We all gathered around closely to watch. She drew directly on the plate with apparent ease and grace. After the drawing was completed, she was whisked away to make a visit to another classroom, but her magic could still be felt in the room. I promised her that I would complete the processing of the plate and contact her when we had finished the printing of the edition. Now, years later, Faith remembers thinking I was crazy and presumptuous to expect her to crank out a drawing without any preparation. Still, she rose to the occasion.

Shortly after Faith's visit, she sent me a thank-you note and said she looked forward to the print. It would be four years before I would deliver it.

During those years, I worked on Faith's *Anyone Can Fly* while building the Experimental Print Institute (EPI) at Lafayette from the fledgling print program. The *Pittsburgh Post-Gazette* described EPI as the "Ink Think Tank," because of its innovative programming and achievements in a number of areas, including exhibitions, visiting artists, international exchanges, and workshops. The mission of the Experimental Printmaking Institute is to provide a creative environment in which professional artists and students can create work and work together to investigate new and experimental approaches to the print medium. EPI offers a student-centered program, where students have direct encounters with established artists, such as Faith and many others. The EPI visiting artist program would grow over the next ten years to bring over fifty professional artists from diverse backgrounds to Lafayette College, resulting in the publication of dozens of print editions, experimental works, and a number of artists' books.

I would return to the *Anyone Can Fly* plate periodically and pull a test proof, then set it away until the next opportunity.

The image is of two small children, Cassie and her younger brother, Be Be, flying over a bridge with the cityscape below. The sky is sprinkled with stars, and the words "Anyone Can Fly" appear just above the bridge's expanse. Faith's signature is in the upper right corner. It is similar to many of her works from that period: *Sonny's Quilt*, 1986, *The Winner*, from Faith's *Woman on a Bridge Series*, 1988, and *Woman Painting the Bay Bridge*, 1988. All are based on Faith's childhood experiences in Harlem. She also recorded many of these early childhood memories in her memoir, *We Flew over the Bridge,* in 1995.

Harlem

"I grew up in Harlem during the Great Depression. This did not mean I was poor and oppressed. We were protected from oppression and surrounded by loving family."

Faith was born on October 8, 1930, at Harlem Hospital in New York City to Andrew Louis Jones and Willie Posey Jones. Harlem, a Mecca for black artists in the 1920's, still remained a place of excitement and creativity, even after the bright lights of the Harlem Renaissance had dimmed. As a young child, Ringgold was often bedridden with asthma, and spent extended periods of time making drawings with the paper and crayons that her mother provided.[1] Willie Posey Jones was a natural teacher and often read to her sick daughter.

Willie believed in self-reliance, and she strongly valued creative expression. These beliefs were passed onto Faith. Her father was a storyteller, who captivated Faith's attention, imagination, and sense of wonderment with his tales of family life in the Harlem community.

The third child in a black working-class family, Faith was expected to achieve more than her parents and to "become somebody." Faith's grandparents had moved from Florida to Harlem during the black migration north early in the twentieth century. During that time, thousands of blacks emigrated to Harlem from rural areas all over the South. "We be goin' up North to a job" was the refrain. Blacks were leaving their homes with hopes of economic opportunities and a chance for their children to escape the segregation and racism of the South.

Faith's parents met in Harlem when they were both sixteen years old. It was 1919 and the height of the Harlem Renaissance. Their early lives personified the quest for a new world full of hope and possibilities. The realities of the Harlem life-—good and bad, real and mythic—became the backdrop for Faith's development as a person and as an artist.[2]

As a child, Faith heard stories about how black people had suffered during their enslavement. She knew that her great-great grandmother had been a slave, but she found it too painful to discuss. For Faith, such stories continued the oral traditions passed down by Africans who had become slaves.

These stories of struggle and triumph over adversity became the impetus for her work, just as the field songs sung by slaves while working on the plantations had served as the foundation of the blues. The blues man's songs told the story of lost love and of a desire for a world that was free of pain and disappointment. The blues man brought the songs of lament from the plantations of the South to the urban black belts of the North.

His songs expressed a desire for freedom and documented the cultural expression of blacks.They also recorded, through words and music, the physical realities of slavery. This oral tradition became the primary means of communicating ideas, emotions, values, and history. Cultural historian Albert Murray describes this phenomenon best: "As for the blues, they affirm not only U.S. Negro life in all its arbitrary complexities and not only life in America in all its infinite confusions, they affirm life and humanity

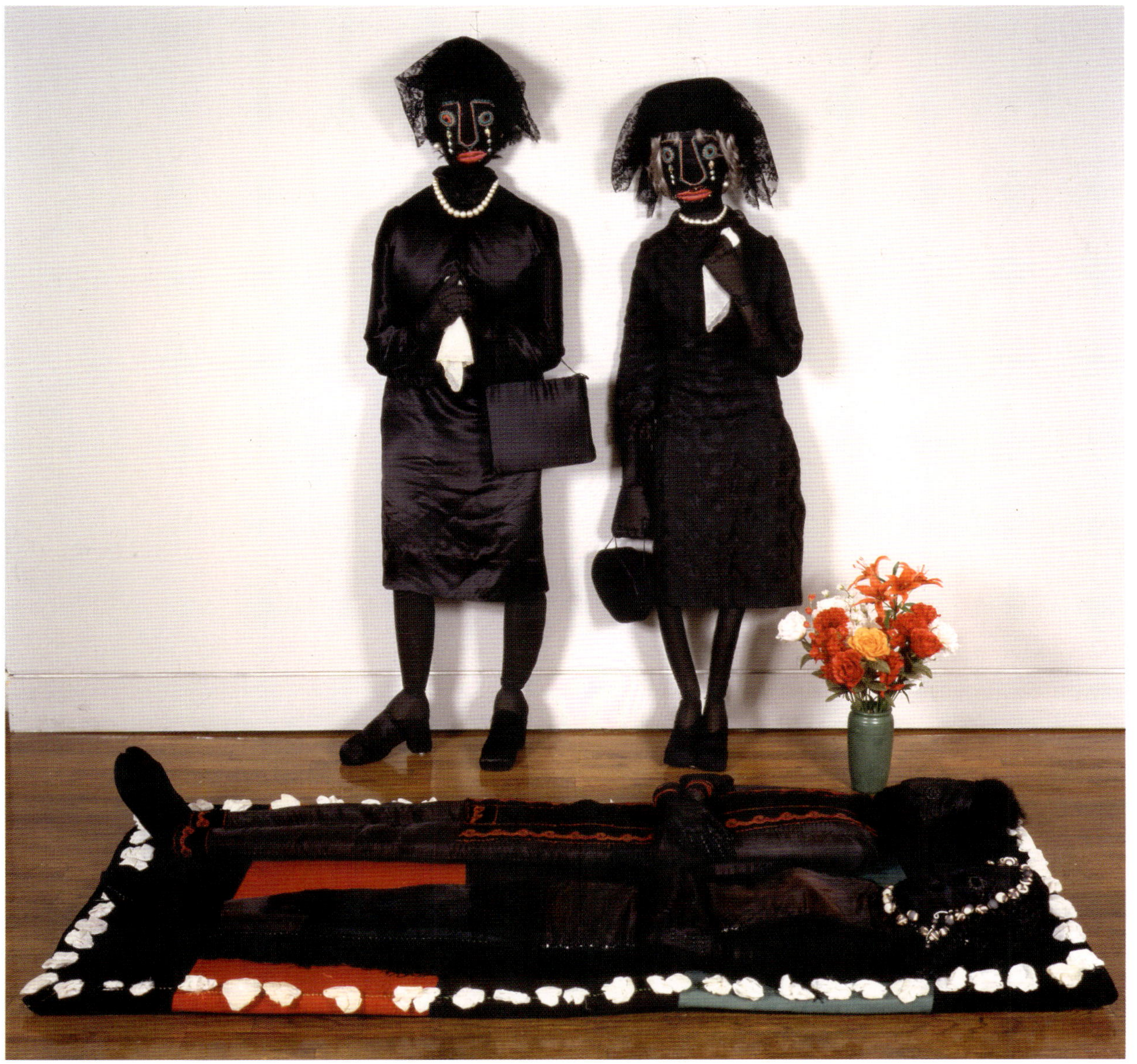

16 The Wake and Resurrection of the Bicentennial Negro, *1976, mixed media installation detail adapted from performance, life size.*

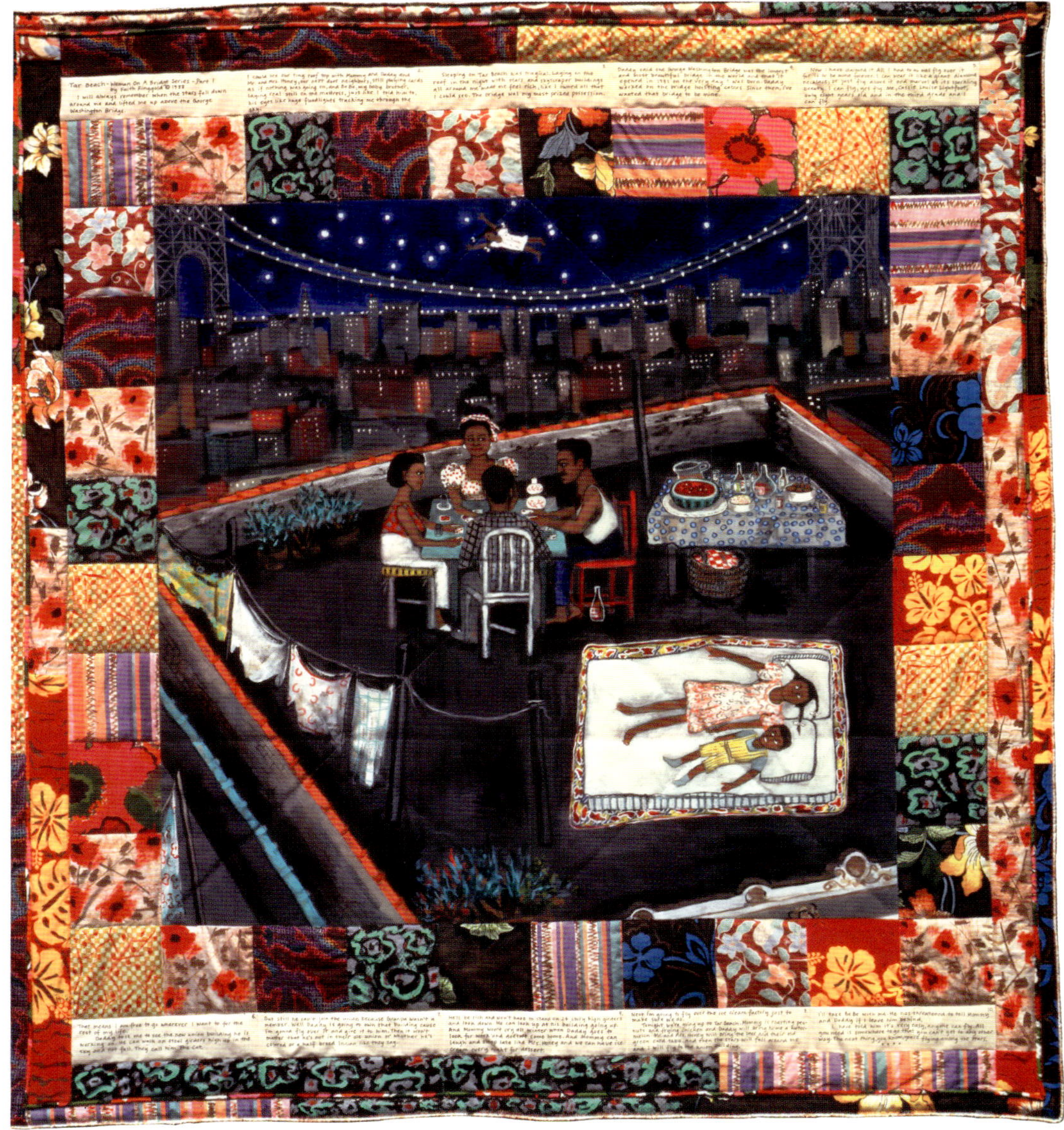

17 Tar Beach: The Woman on a Bridge Series #1, *1988, acrylic on canvas; printed, tie-dyed, painted, and pieced fabric, 74 x 69 in.*

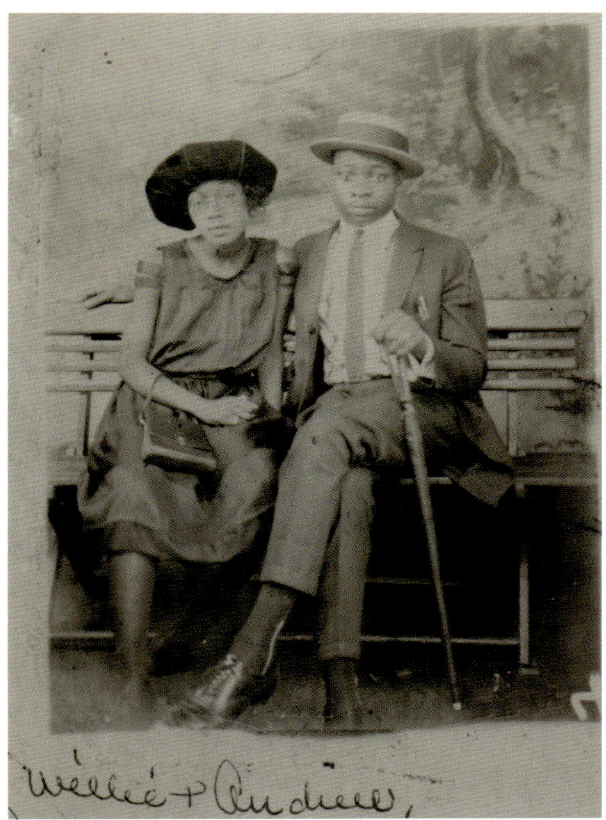

18 *Willie Posey and Andrew Jones, Jr., Faith's parents, 1920.*

itself in the very process of confronting failures and existentialistic absurdities. The spirit of the blues moves in the opposite direction from ashes and sack-cloth, self-pity, self-hatred, and suicide."[3] For Faith, these traditions took on heroic significance and have continued to be subjects of her art and research.

Although Faith was born ten years after the golden decade of the Harlem Renaissance, she grew up with its legacy. The heroes of the Harlem Renaissance represented the story of the "New Negro," who replaced the shame of slavery with a pride of accomplishment. The stories of achievement were for the most part about the music and literature created by legendary figures, such as composer and bandleader Duke Ellington and writer Langston Hughes. These renowned individuals and others like them lived just around the corner from Faith's family. Faith's first husband was an up-and-coming musician who befriended many young performers, including the noted Sonny Rollins and the legendary Miles Davis.

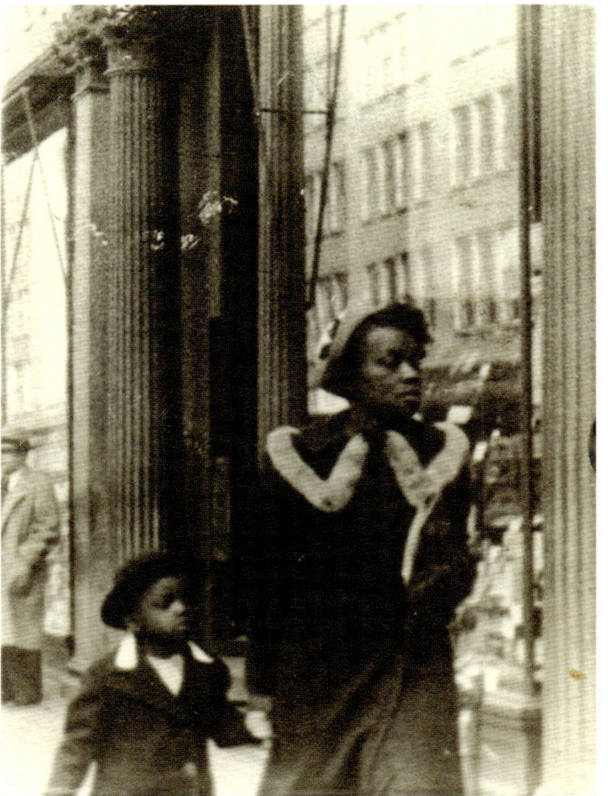

19 *Faith with her mother, 1933.*

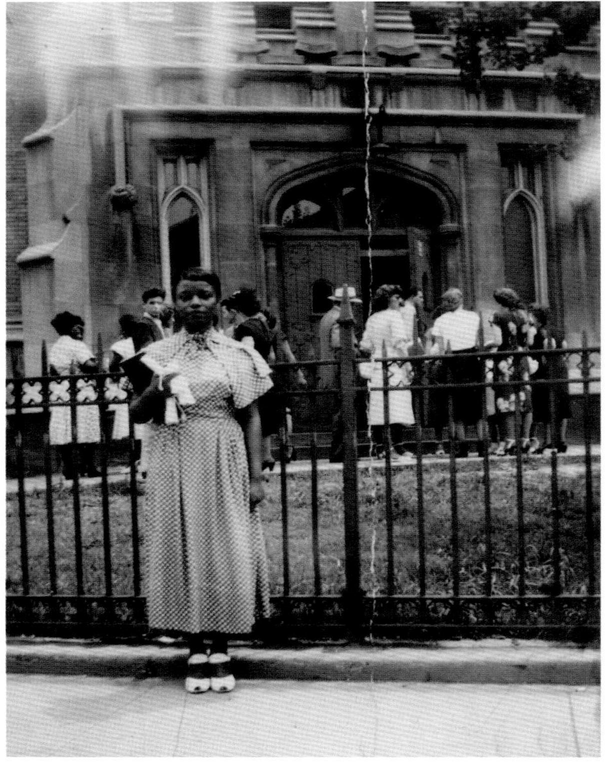

20 *Faith at graduation from high school, 1948.*

Sonny became Faith's close friend and a symbol of what an artist could be like. He often came to visit her parents, who entertained friends and extended family on a regular basis. Sonny once played a special song for Faith at her birthday party. She told me of how he would always have his horn with him, and that she often heard him practicing from her bedroom window. Through that same window Faith could see the George Washington Bridge, a massive structure with draping cables. As a child, she often imagined that the bridge was the magic highway to the rest of the world.

Faith has confessed to me that while this period of her life was full of excitement, it was sometimes intruded on by the ugliness of the world around her. Ringgold was very proud of her family, and carried herself with pride and confidence. But at school she was less sure. She began to think about what she wanted to do with her life; however, the overt segregation she had witnessed in her school was sobering. She began to think about her future as a black person. She was a very good student who was taught always to be respectful of others and to carry herself with pride, but she was aware that the world of school was not the same as the safer world created by her loving parents, and she approached it with a measure of caution. Her family's expectation was that she would go to college, but her teachers—who were almost all white— had other ideas about what she should be and told her otherwise. Faith relied on her parents to know the truth and what was best for her. "I trusted them," she told me, "not like some children today."

I sometimes think that Faith and I were probably destined to meet one way or another. Before coming to Lafayette College in 1991, I had a National Endowment Fellowship to work with master printmaker Bob Blackburn at the prominent Printmaking Workshop in New York City. After I completed my fellowship, I continued to visit Bob in the following years and valued his mentorship.

Blackburn had established his workshop in 1948, and it would become the oldest operating nonprofit print workshop in the country until its demise in 2001. I mentioned Faith's participation in Lafayette's artist-in-residence program to Bob, and this prompted him to show me a number of Faith's earlier prints.

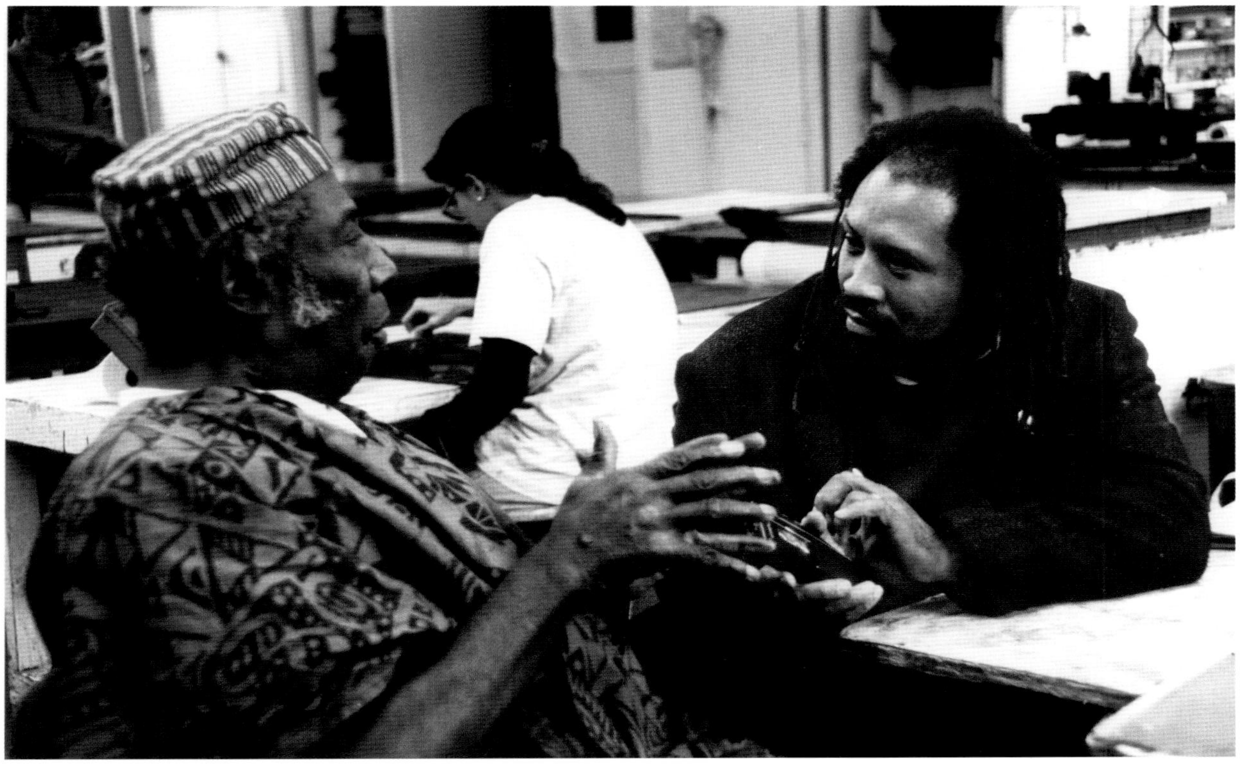

21 *Robert Blackburn and Curlee R. Holton at Printmaking Workshop in New York City, 1994.*

Blackburn greatly admired Faith, and spoke highly of her success as an artist. He found it remarkable that Faith had worked as a teacher for almost twenty years but never had stopped showing or promoting her art. "She has more determination than any artist that I've ever met." he told me.

Later, after telling Faith that I had worked with Blackburn, Faith laughed softly as she told me that she had made her first real print with Blackburn. She explained that her college printmaking experience was a disaster. She hated printmaking so passionately that she was always the one who volunteered to get the class coffee so she could escape. Faith had told Blackburn the story of her early disappointment with the experience of printmaking, and he invited her to come and print with him. Bob was remarkably persuasive. She made nine different prints in a single year (1988) with Blackburn, including important works such as *The Death of Apartheid, Slave Rape, No More War,* and *Women, Power, Poverty, and Love*. Her last print with Blackburn would be her donation to the workshop, titled *Under a Blood Red Sky*, 2000.

THE ARTIST/PRINTER RELATIONSHIP

In 1997, I delivered the *Anyone Can Fly* print to Faith, at her home in Englewood, New Jersey. I had called first to make an appointment and arrived on time at Faith's residence on a beautiful, tree-lined street of large, well-appointed homes. I was struck by the difference between this house, a beautifully landscaped contemporary red brick, and the stark white studio I had visited years before in New York City. I would later learn that Faith had carefully drawn up her wish list when she decided to build the studio: natural light, large windows, northern exposure, a bedroom so she could nap during an intense work session if she chose, a bathroom, a kitchen, office space, and plenty of pure white walls. Her studio was designed by architect Aaron Kramer, who added a skylight, which focused daylight directly onto her main work area.

Before entering the driveway to her home, I had to navigate the security system and the large wrought-iron gate. After slowly pulling into the drive, trimmed with plants and a hand-crafted birdhouse, I pulled to a stop and stepped out with some trepidation, clutching my portfolio of prints.

As I approached the front door I was warmly greeted by Faith's husband, Birdie, who ushered me into the living room. As I waited for Faith, I looked around at the walls, covered by large brightly colored abstract hangings and posters from her many exhibitions. One painting was composed of jagged shapes of reds, blues, and greens. A sewn border of the same canvas lent a unified yet dynamic element to the work. The painting also had raffia hanging from the bottom, which made it appear more like a sculpture hanging from the wall than a painting. I was to see another similar work titled *Dah #3* as I climbed the stairs to the second-floor studio. I recalled that I had seen these works reproduced in Faith's memoirs.

I continued to look around and surprisingly encountered two large soft-sculpture dolls with round chocolate faces and button eyes. They had long pigtails and wore yellow dresses with large red dots, and were placed at the glass dining room table as if they were

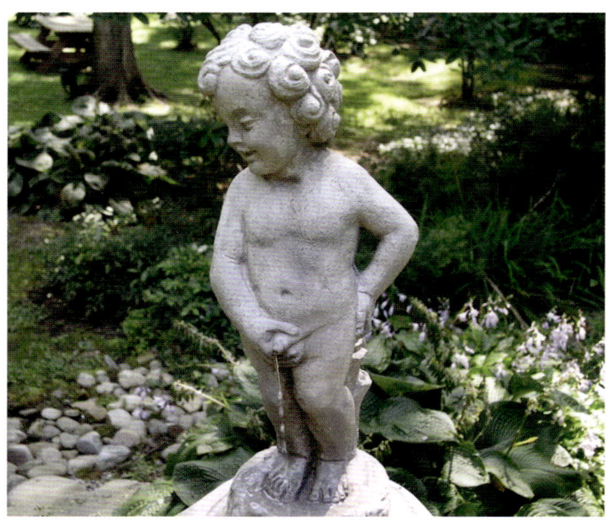

22 *Mannequin Pis in Faith's garden.*

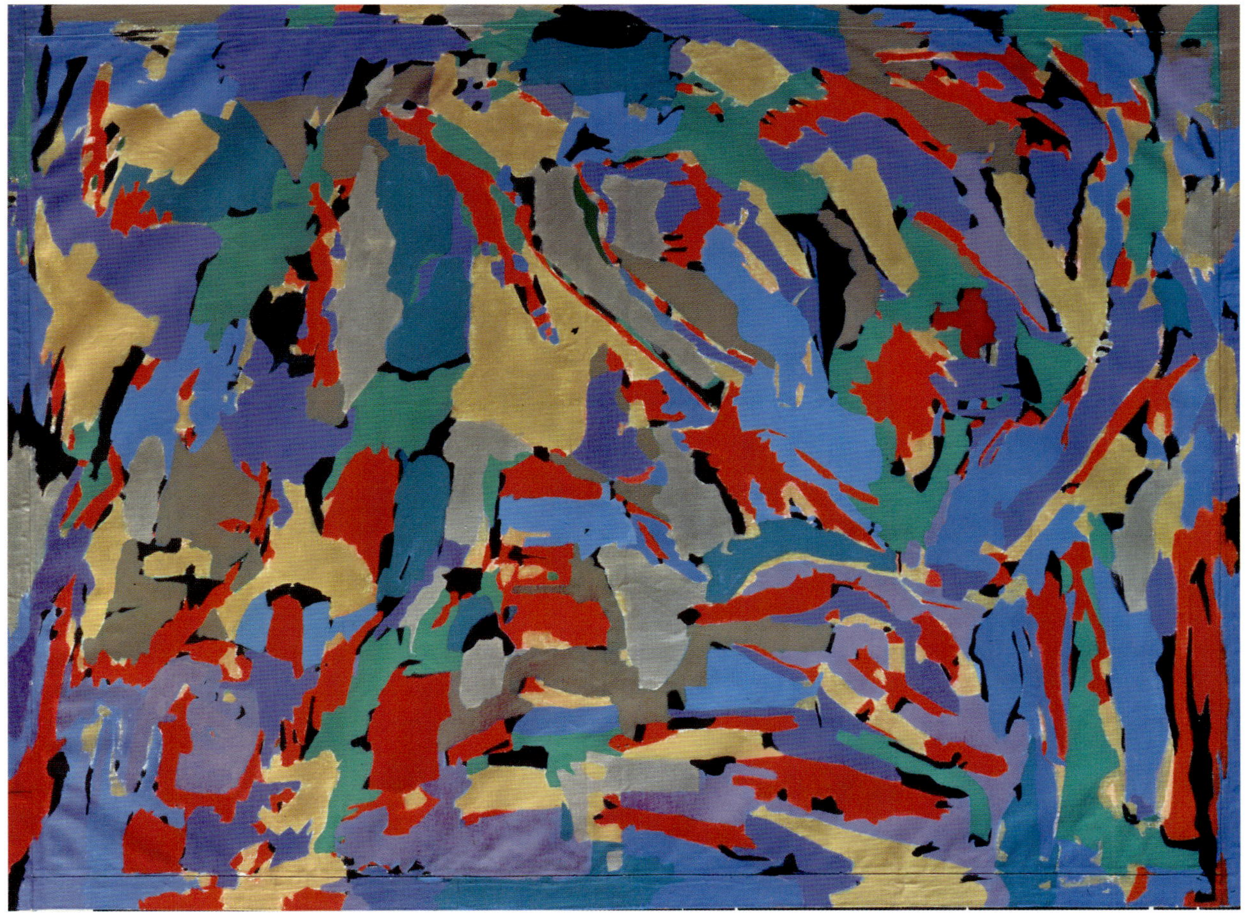

23 Dah #3, *1983, acrylic on canvas, 72 x 54 in.*

having afternoon tea. Shortly after, Faith entered from a rear room and invited me to join her in the studio. As we walked toward the stairs leading to the studio we passed large plate-glass windows that separated the house from a magical garden full of flowers, exotic plants, and a pond full of fish adorned with a fountain of the famous Belgian sculpture *Mannequin Pis*.

After we became reacquainted, Faith showed me around her studio and talked about her new work and how much she enjoyed her visit to Lafayette. While listening to her every word, my eyes darted from painting to painting. I presented her with the *Anyone Can Fly* print. She was quite pleased with the overall quality, especially my choice to print it in sepia ink.

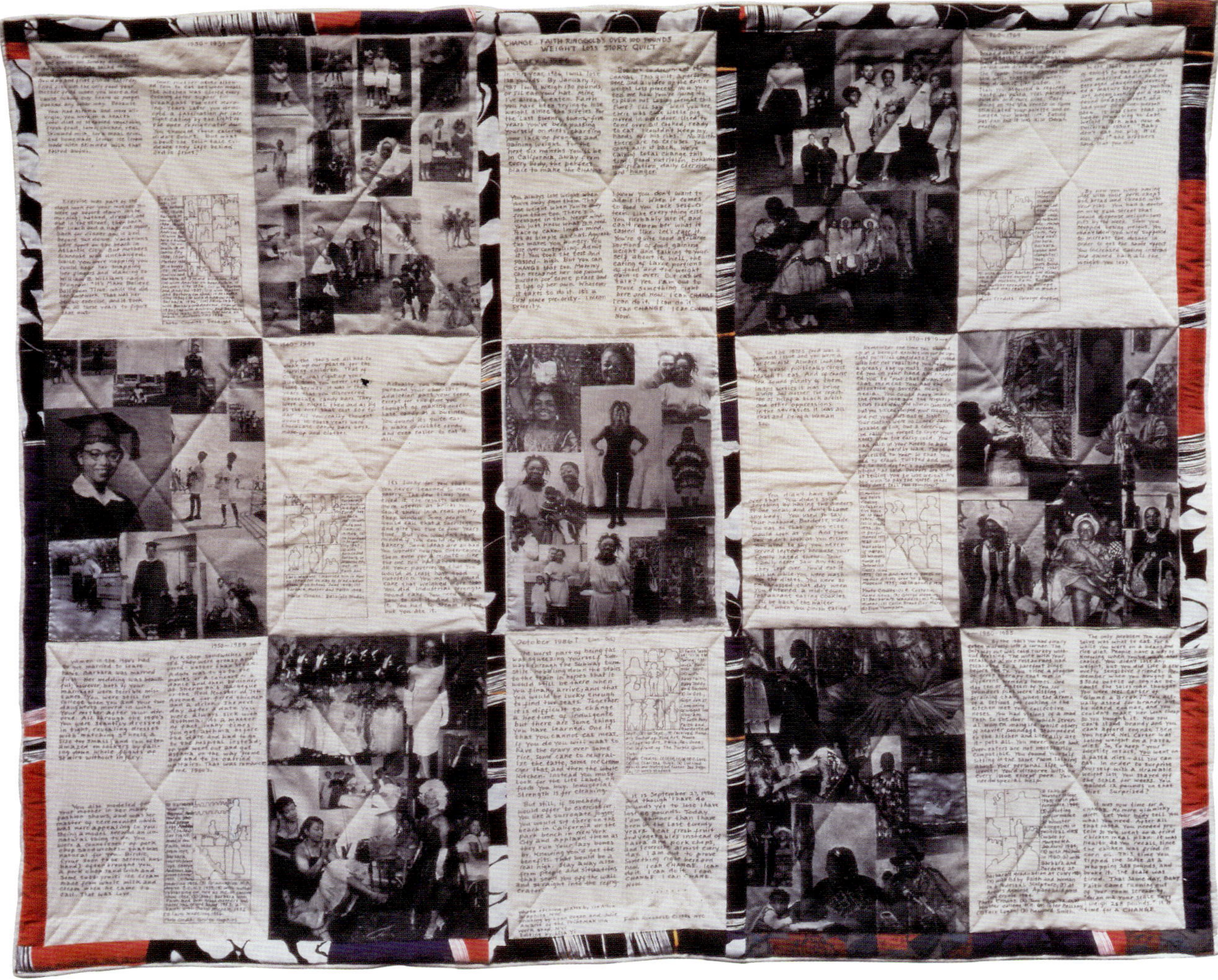

24 Change: Faith Ringgold's Over 100 Pound Weight Loss Performance Story Quilt: Change Series #1, *1986, photo etching on silk and cotton; printed and pieced fabric, 57½ x 70¼ in.*

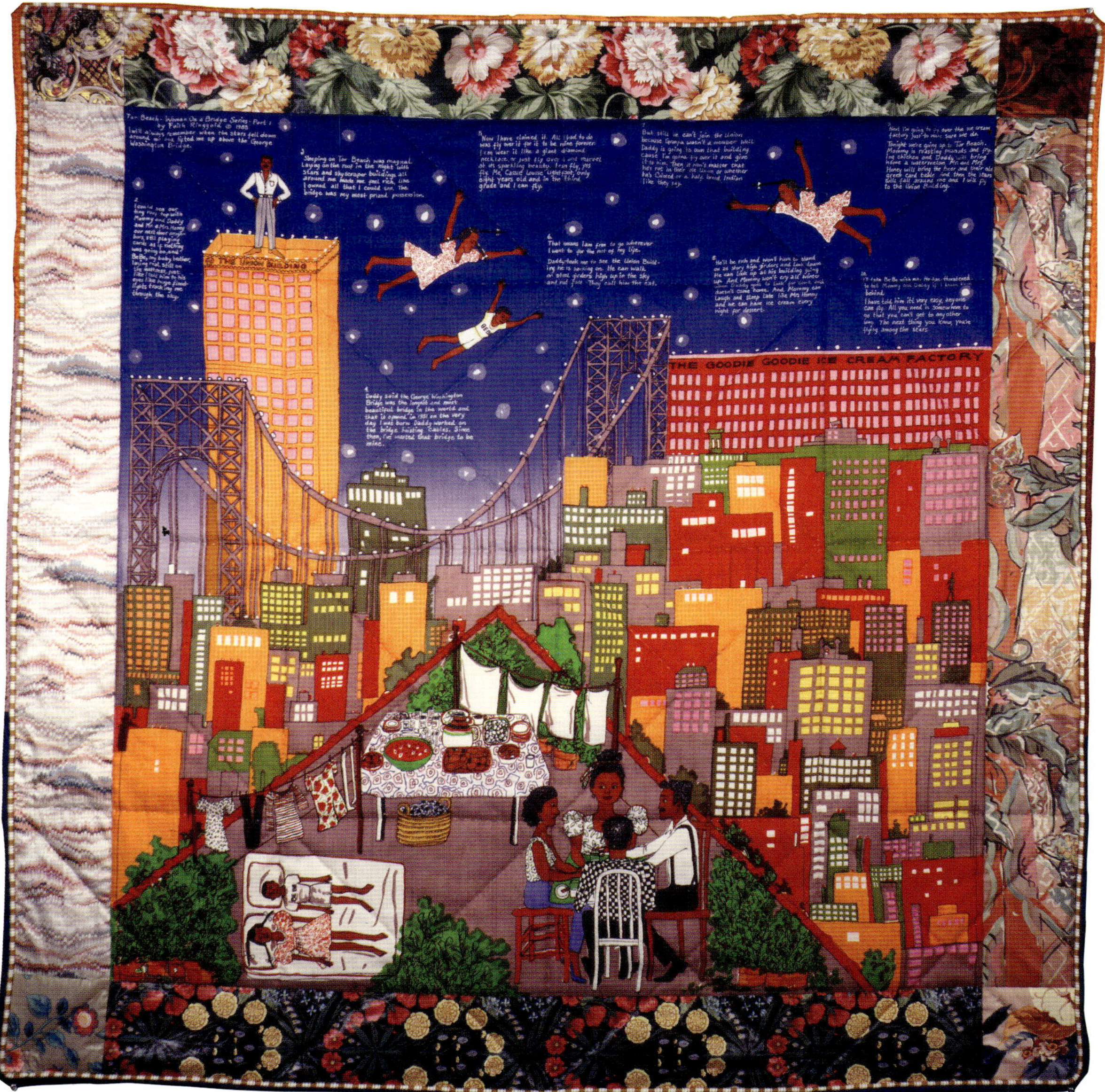

25 Tar Beach 2, *1990, silk screen on silk, 68 x 64 in.*

Faith signed each print and inscribed an artist proof to me with the words, "You can fly and make prints, too."

The edition of twenty for *Anyone Can Fly* was small in comparison to some of the editions Faith had printed with other printers to that point. She had also experimented with various print mediums in the making of her quilts and other objects. She had made photo-etched plates that were printed directly onto panels in her piece *Change: Faith Ringgold's Over 100 Pound Weight Loss Performance Story Quilt*, made in 1986. She had also used the screen-printing process in the making of her *Tar Beach 2* quilt in 1990 at the Fabric Workshop in Philadelphia, Pennsylvania.[4]

Faith did not restrict her images to just one medium. For example, her work *Joe Baker's Birthday* from her *French Collections Series,Part II, #9* was made first as a quilt in 1993, and printed as a serigraph print in 1995.

We created a number of prints throughout the years that were based on her major paintings, such as the second print I made with her, *We Came To America*, in 1998.

This image was first sketched out by Faith at her studio and then drawn directly onto the plate in the same manner that she had drawn *Anyone Can Fly*. The plate was then sent back to my studio, where it was etched and proofed.

After I made a number of proofs, I returned to her studio, where she approved one of the test prints for editioning. The final image was printed in eleven different colors on a single plate. I learned this technique of applying multiple colors on a single plate rather than creating a separate plate for each color while studying with master printmakers at the Taller de

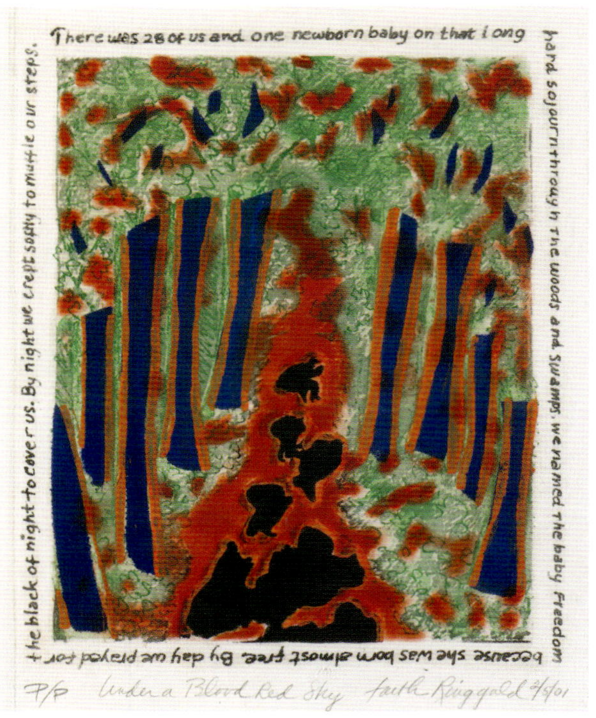

26 Under a Blood Red Sky, *color etching, 15 x 18 in.*

Artes Plasticas Rufino Tamayo in Oaxaca, Mexico. This technique of color application allows details and surface qualities to be retained even though only one plate is used that has been inked and wiped multiple times. The results are richly colored images with a surface sensuality that makes the hours of labor required for the printing of each impression well worth it.

When I finished printing the edition, I contacted Faith, who was teaching at the University of California in San Diego, where she had been since 1985.

Faith invited me and my wife to visit her at her studio in La Jolla, California, where she signed the edition.

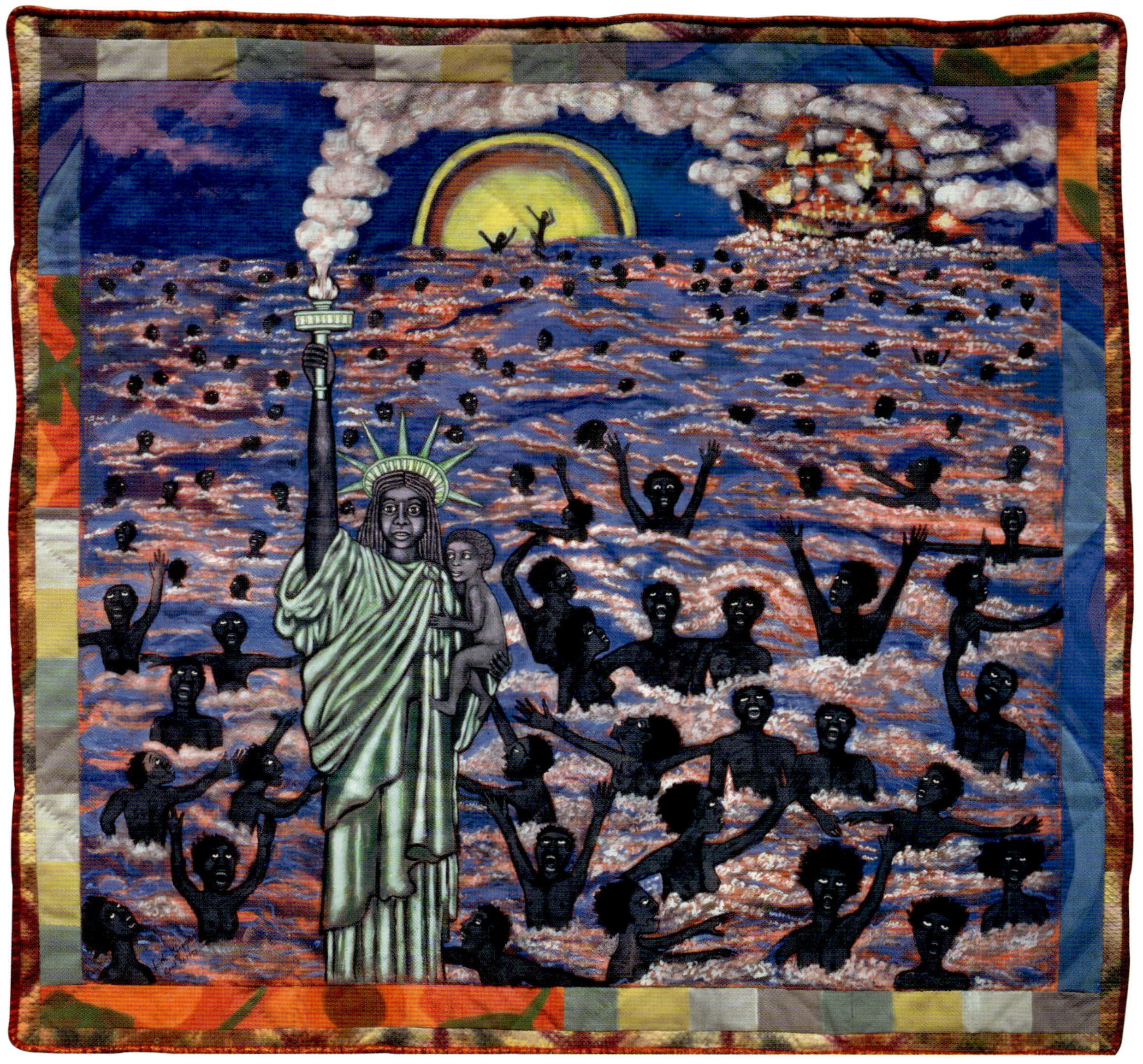

27 We Came to America: The American Collection: #1, *1997, acrylic on canvas; painted, tie-dyed, and pieced fabric, 74½ x 79½ in.*

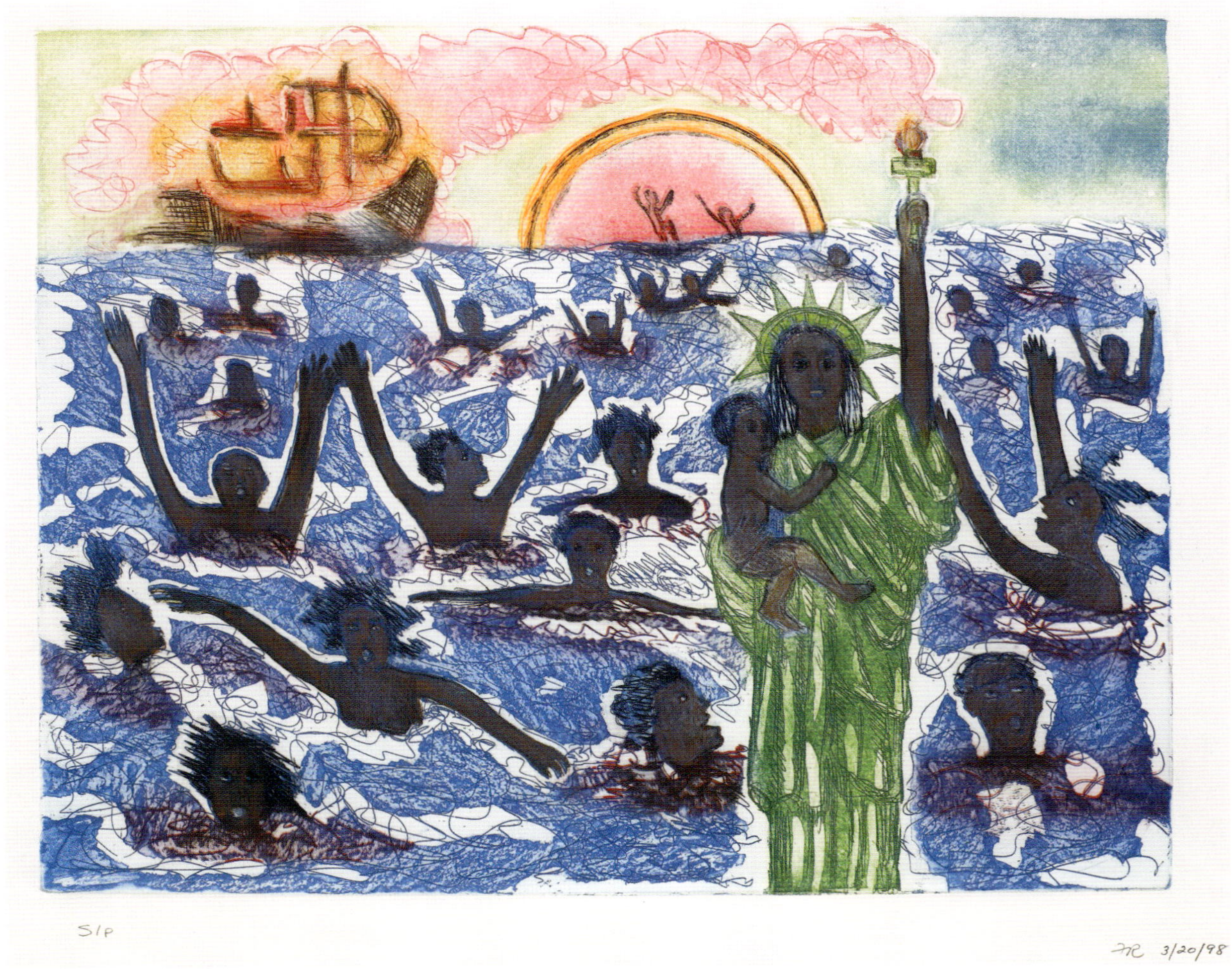

28 We Came to America, *1998, color etching, 22 x 30 in.*

Although we had collaborated on a number of ideas for other prints and trial proofs, this project seemed to cement our relationship. I had become the master printer, and we had become collaborators.

Next, Faith and I collaborated on a print to support Bob Blackburn's Printmaking Workshop. She and a number of well-known artists from around the country had been invited to create original prints, which would be sold to raise crucial funds needed to keep the doors of the workshop open. Faith decided

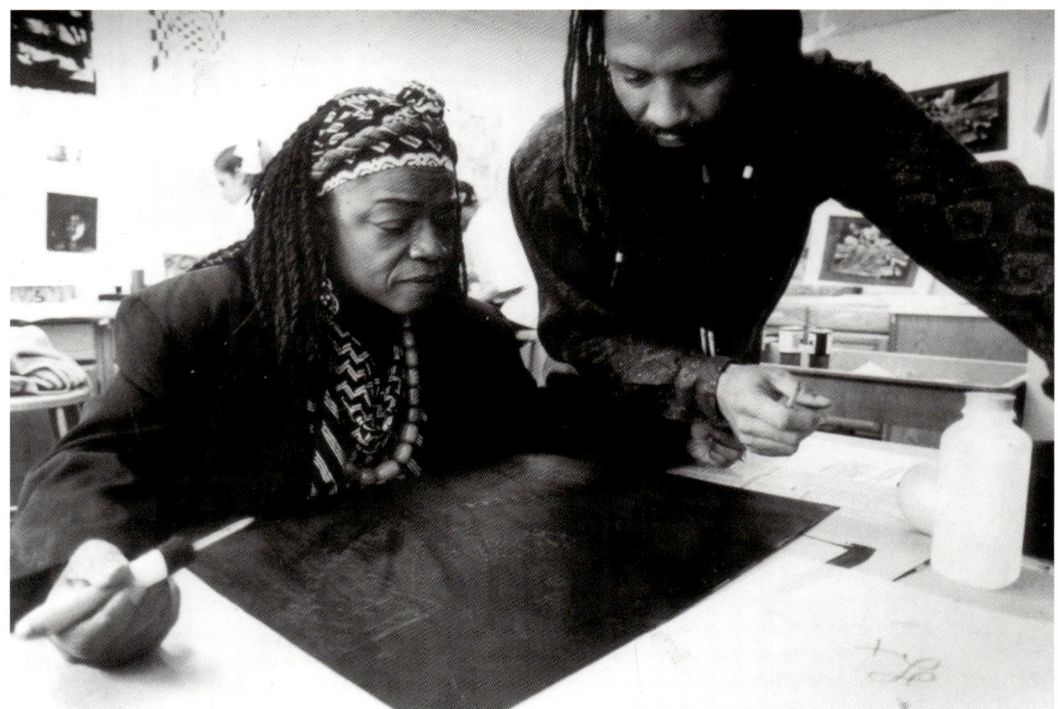

29 Faith Ringgold and Curlee Holton working on a plate at EPI.

that she would make a print from her new *Jones Road Series*. The print was editioned and sold to help the workshop; however, all efforts failed. Sadly, it finally closed its doors in 2001 after fifty-three years of continuous operation, making it the oldest non-profit workshop in America.

During my many visits to Faith's studio, we would often speak of Blackburn and his contribution to printmaking and the legacy of African American art. We reflected on the workshop experience and how it had influenced our own work, as well as the powerful dynamic that occurs when practicing artists share the same space. Both Faith and I met many famous artists while working at

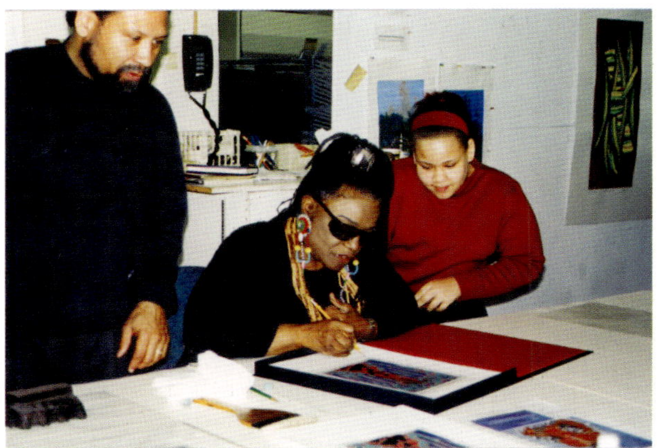

30 Curlee Holton, Faith Ringgold, and Ananda Holton, February 5, 2001.

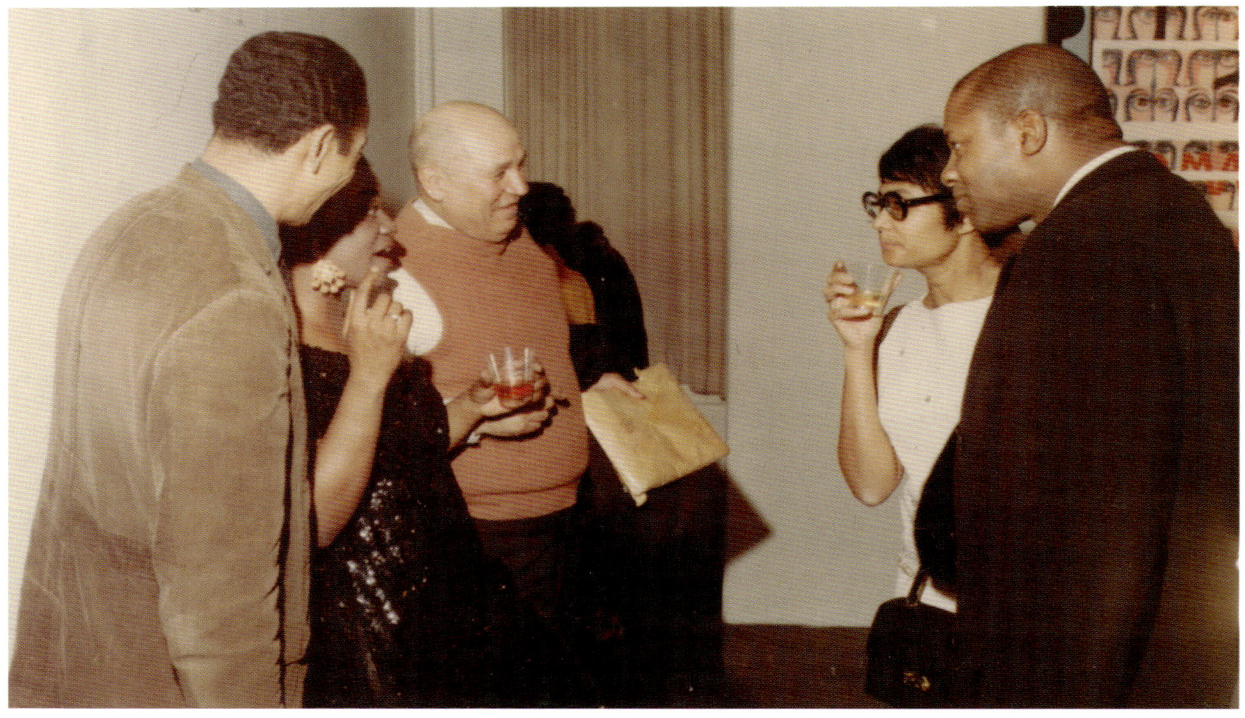

31 *Faith's first solo show at the Spectrum Gallery on 57th Street, New York City, 1967.*

Bob's, some of whom were Faith's contemporaries, including Emma Amos and Romare Bearden, whom Faith admired greatly. Bearden, Norman Lewis, Ernest Chriclow, and Richard Mayhew supported Faith by attending her first solo show at the Spectrum Gallery in New York City in 1967. Their presence was an important endorsement of Faith's work. A number of art critics were in attendance as well. In the February 1968 issue of *Arts Magazine*, John Fisher wrote about Faith Ringgold's "American People" exhibition: "Although self consciously ambitious, these paintings show exceptional talent. The artist has a penetrating sense of irony, which she graphically translates into pictorial emotion effectively."[5]

The encouraging reviews and the large turnout for her 1967 show were important factors in establishing Ringgold's reputation as a new and powerful voice on the art scene. She represented a clear departure from the European-inspired classicism of Bearden's collages and Mayhew's Hudson River School-influenced landscapes. Ringgold personified a new generation of artists—bold and experimental—who also functioned as political advocates. In some ways, her work recalled the traditions of Francisco Goya and Pablo Picasso—artists who felt a deep sense of public responsibility.

COLLABORATIONS—PAST AND PRESENT

"During the 1970s it wasn't enough to deal with blackness. The feminist in me had to be addressed.... I took a chance and it was the best thing I had ever done."

Faith decided she wanted me to reprint *Under a Blood Red Sky*, adding three additional plates—one to add an additional green, another to add a bold black line, which would better define the image, and the third to add a relief effect to the final print. This was the first of her prints on which I would include her signature text around the borders. When *Under a Blood Red Sky* was signed, I had the pleasure of hosting Faith at my studio.

The print program had moved from the small residence into a spacious studio that had once served as a storage building for the college. In addition to Faith's scheduled signing of the print, she gave a reading and book signing at the college library. We also invited guests to the studio to watch her print.

Garden Party #1 was our next endeavor, published to document the annual garden party Faith hosted at her home to benefit her Anyone Can Fly Foundation. The woman who once longed to fly beyond her bedroom window and over the George Washington Bridge now had a lush garden complete with landscaped paths and bubbling brooks.

But the garden is only a vehicle for her real passion, the Anyone Can Fly Foundation. Faith established the foundation with the intention of expanding the established art canon to include artists of the African Diaspora and to introduce those artists and art traditions to children and adults. Her foundation received its official non-profit status in 2002 and distributes

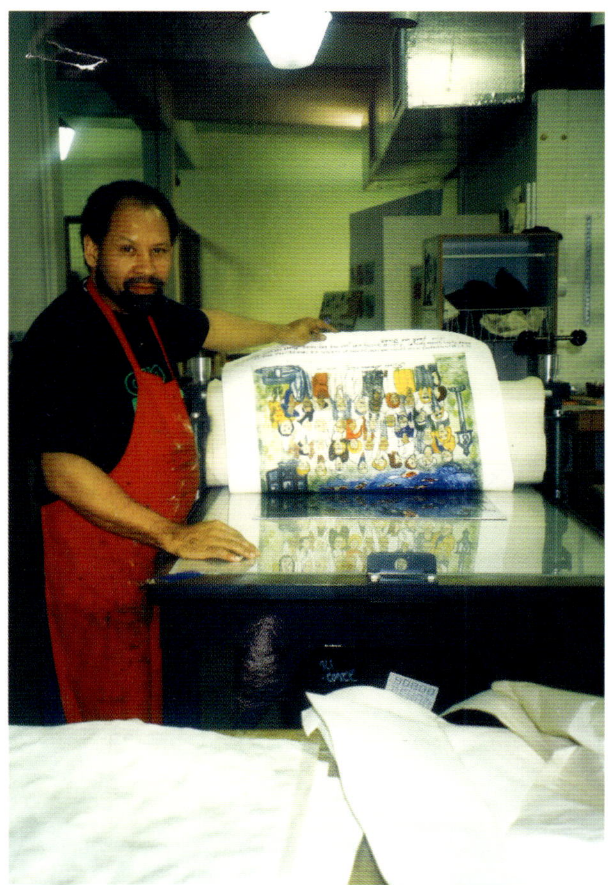

32 *Curlee Holton pulling proof print of* Garden Party #1, *April 2001.*

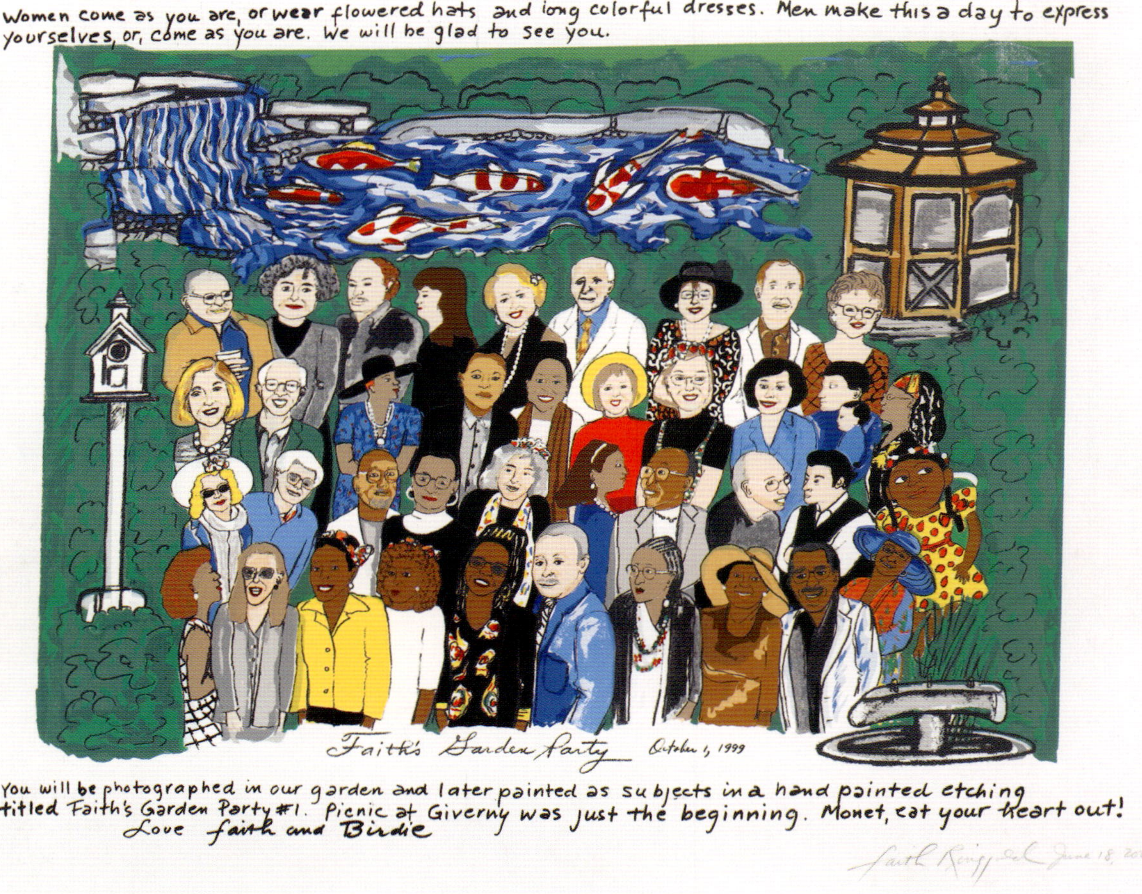

33 Garden Party #1, *June 15, 2001, serigraph, 22 x 30 in.*

fellowships to young scholars, allowing them to write about the works of artists, such as Lois Mailou Jones, Romare Bearden, Robert Blackburn, and Richmond Barthe.

Garden Party #1 records the important guests who helped Faith celebrate the foundation's conception. Many of these friends are fellow artists and gallery owners, who promoted Faith's works when she had little support, particularly when she took on controversial issues, such as race and women's liberation.

Faith's feminist work, which had been fermenting since the start of her career, surfaced strongly in the 1960s. An early example of her focus on the female as subject can be seen in her 1967 work *Soul Sister*.

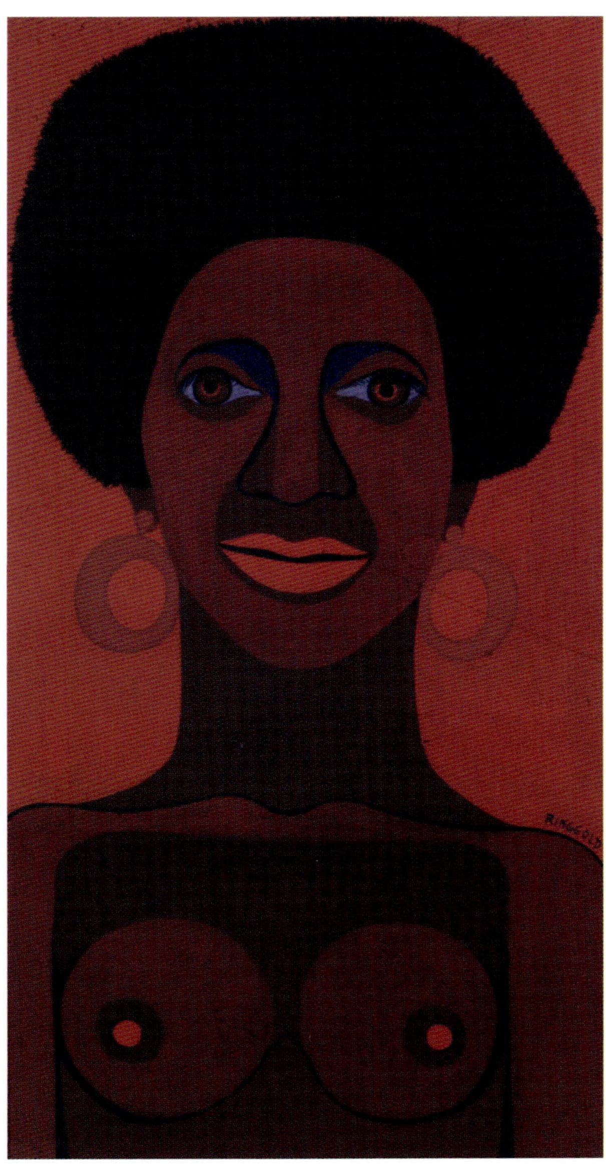

34 Soul Sister: The Black Light Series #3, *1967, oil on canvas, 36 x 18 in.*

This oil on canvas portrays a determined, young black woman with an Afro hairstyle, worn like a warrior's helmet. Her large lips and nose assert a new vision of beauty that embraces the sculptural archetypes of Africa. Her hoop earrings remind us of the adornment of young Nubian women preparing for a rite of passage into adulthood. Her breasts appear firm and upright, with erect nipples that signal her fertility.

A number of early works on the walls of Faith's studio remind the viewer of her singular message in other works from this period. The *Ego Painting* of 1969 asserts that the black woman should not be left out of the struggle for liberation, as does *Between Friends*, 1963, from her *American People Series*.

Faith's focus on feminist issues is closely linked to race. For her, the two subjects are inseparable. Faith told me that she was raised in a household where women were the "masters" of their own fates. In her family, women could not and would not accept anything less.

From 1960 until the late 1970s, Faith sold very little work. Although she received a great deal of attention, collectors and institutions were uncomfortable with her images. She had to work hard to overcome the rejection and neglect that she and other black artists felt and that women faced in the broader society.[6]

She and others organized a public protest in front of the Whitney Museum of American Art on the occasion of a 1968 exhibition celebrating painting and sculpture from the 1930s. The show failed to include any black artists. Even Jacob Lawrence, a black artist in the Whitney's permanent collection, was excluded.[7]

More protest activity led to Faith's arrest on November 13, 1970. Her flag paintings were included in "The People's Flag Show" exhibit at the Judson Memorial Church in Greenwich Village, organized by

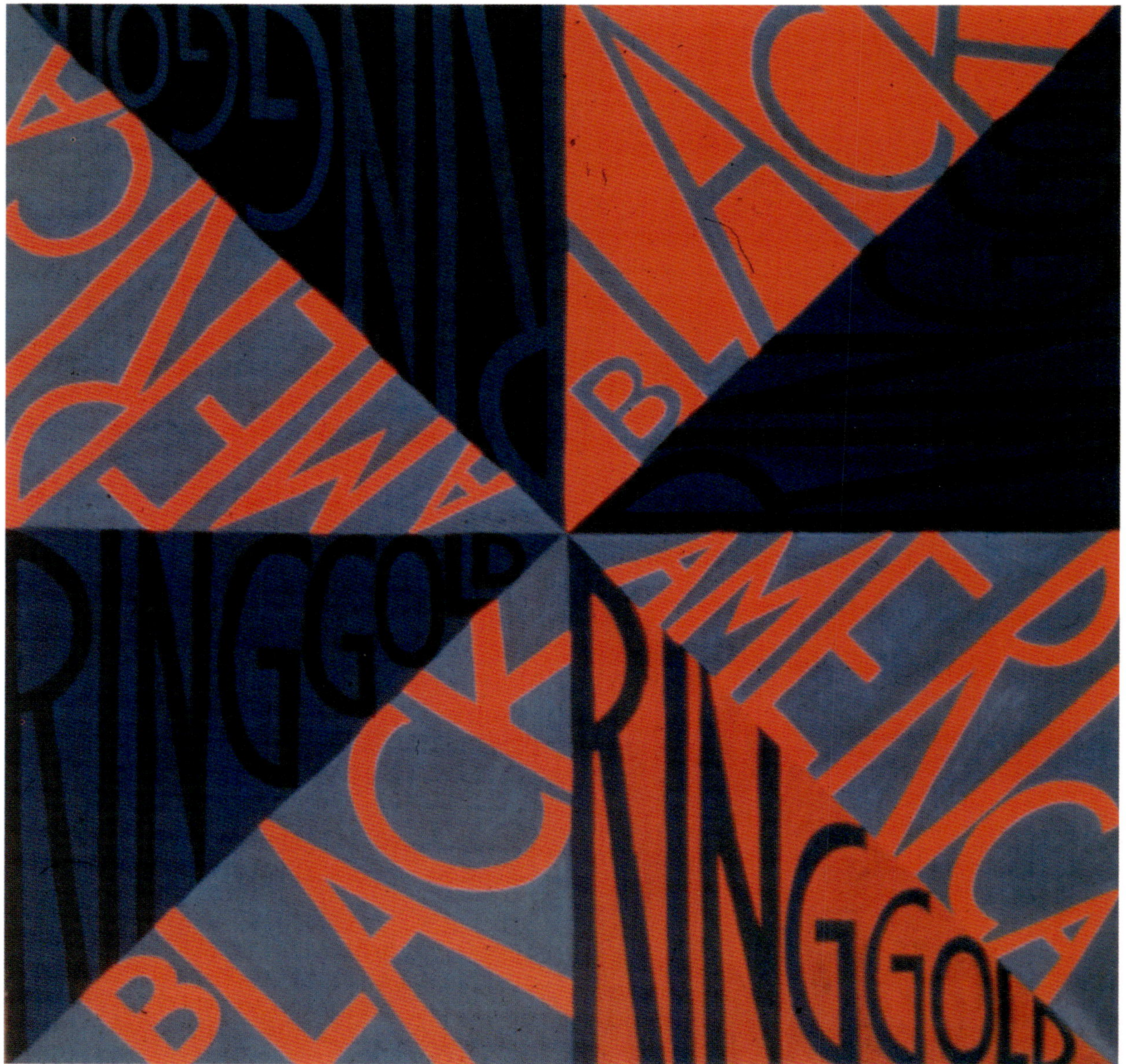

 35 Ego Painting: The Black Light Series #7, *1969, oil on canvas, 30 x 30 in.*

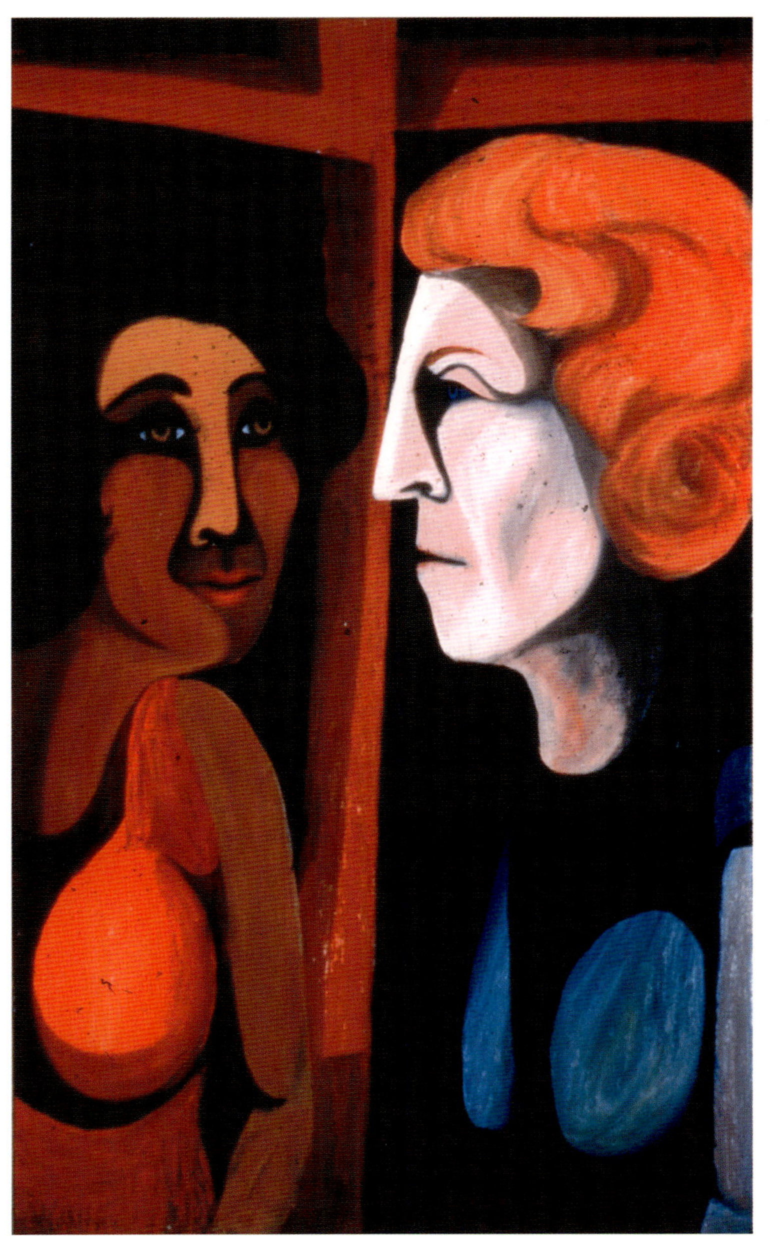

36 Between Friends: The American People Series #1, *1963, oil on canvas, 40 x 24 in.*

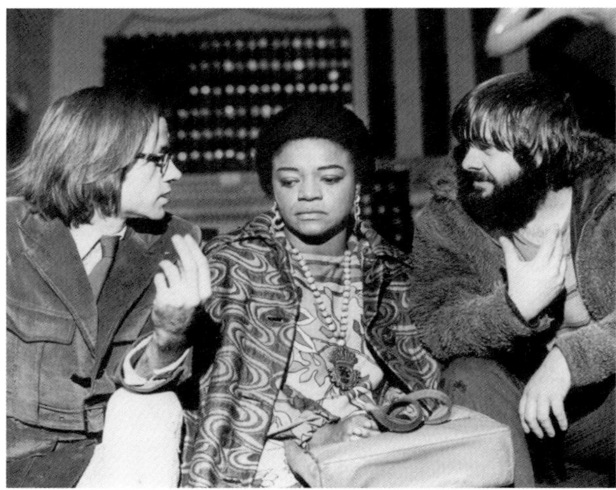

37 The Judson 3: Jean Toche, Faith Ringgold, and Jon Hendricks at 'The People's Flag Show,' New York, 1970.

a group of independent artists to protest oppression both in the United States and abroad. Faith was a member of the show's organizing committee and was apprehended along with fellow organizers Jean Toche and Jon Hendricks. Their arrest for "desecration of the flag" served to bring the show to an end. Although horrified at being charged with a crime, Faith felt that she and the other members of the People's Flag Show Committee had made a much larger point—art needed to address injustices and oppression.

Faith went to Europe in the summer of 1972 with her daughter, Michele. While Michele went off to visit some friends in Spain, Faith went to see the Documenta art exhibition in Kassel, Germany.

On that trip, Faith worked on a new series of landscape watercolors aptly entitled *Political Landscapes*. These works contained politically inspired texts written vertically on each image, similar to the writing in Chinese landscape paintings.[8]

Michele contributed eight texts for paintings in the series, but Faith authored the other forty-nine, all of which focus on racism in the United States and the relationships between black men and black women.

Later, Faith would note that this was the beginning of her inclusion of actual written text in her work and perhaps the beginning of her formal career as a writer.

Faith's visit to the Rijksmuseum in Amsterdam, where she encountered a collection of Tibetan and Nepali paintings from the fourteenth and fifteenth centuries, would prove to be a critically important experience. There, Faith closely examined the ancient cloth brocade that framed each painting.

She had found yet another way that she could display her work, without the expense of shipping heavy crated and framed paintings. She decided that she could hang her work directly on the wall.

These *tankas* inspired her to include beautiful fabrics along the borders of her paintings.[9]

Faith returned to the studio soon after her trip to Europe to prepare for her first retrospective exhibition. While doing so, she began to collaborate with her mother on a new body of work that would incorporate elements from the Tibetan *tankas* she had seen in Amsterdam. This new series was entitled *Slave Rape*. In these works Ringgold imagines what it would have been like had she been an African woman captured and sold into slavery in America. Faith drew on the oral tradition of slaves in America and she drew on her own research, but perhaps most importantly, she reached deep inside herself and let her feelings as a mother, as a daughter, and as a woman give her the words and the images for the experience.

Faith invited her mother, Willie Posey, to collaborate with her on this project. Ringgold's mother had been a popular clothing designer in Harlem in the 1950s and 1960s, creating unique apparel for the black elite of Harlem. An expert in fabrics and a noted seamstress, she was more than happy to assist her daughter. Ringgold had always considered Willie her closest friend and role model. If she was going to collaborate with anyone it would naturally be her mother.[10]

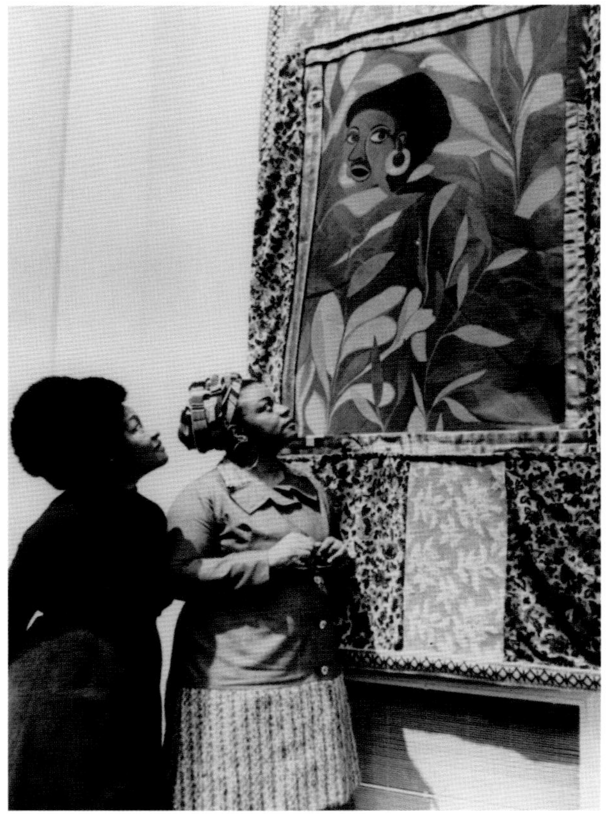

38 Ringgold and her mother in an art gallery, viewing the tanka *Run: The Slave Rape Series*, 1973.

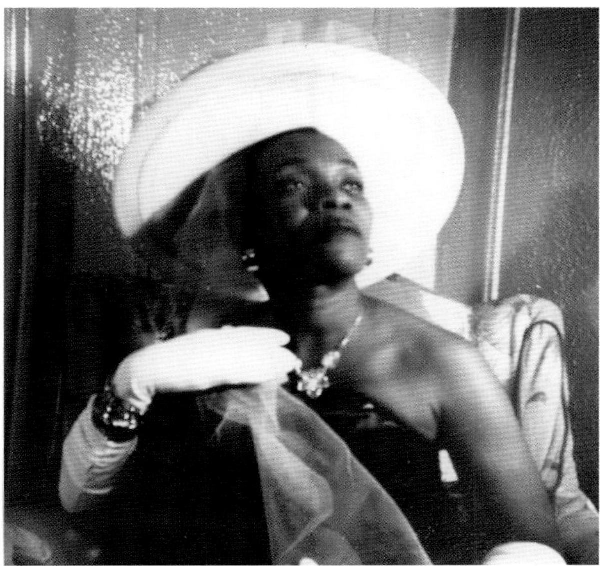

39 Faith's mother posing, 1945.

This mother-daughter collaboration produced some of Ringgold's most important work and eventually led to the making of their first quilt together in 1980.

I never had the opportunity to meet Faith's mother, but her spirit is still very much alive in Faith's work. In 1983 Faith made a special quilt titled *Mother's Quilt* in honor of their collaboration and love for one another.

In between teaching and producing my own work, I labored on *Garden Party #1*, which took almost a full year to complete. I initially developed the image as an etched plate from one of Faith's drawings and printed it as we had printed *We Came To America*. However, Faith was never quite pleased with any of the proofs and is an exacting critic of anything that bears her name.

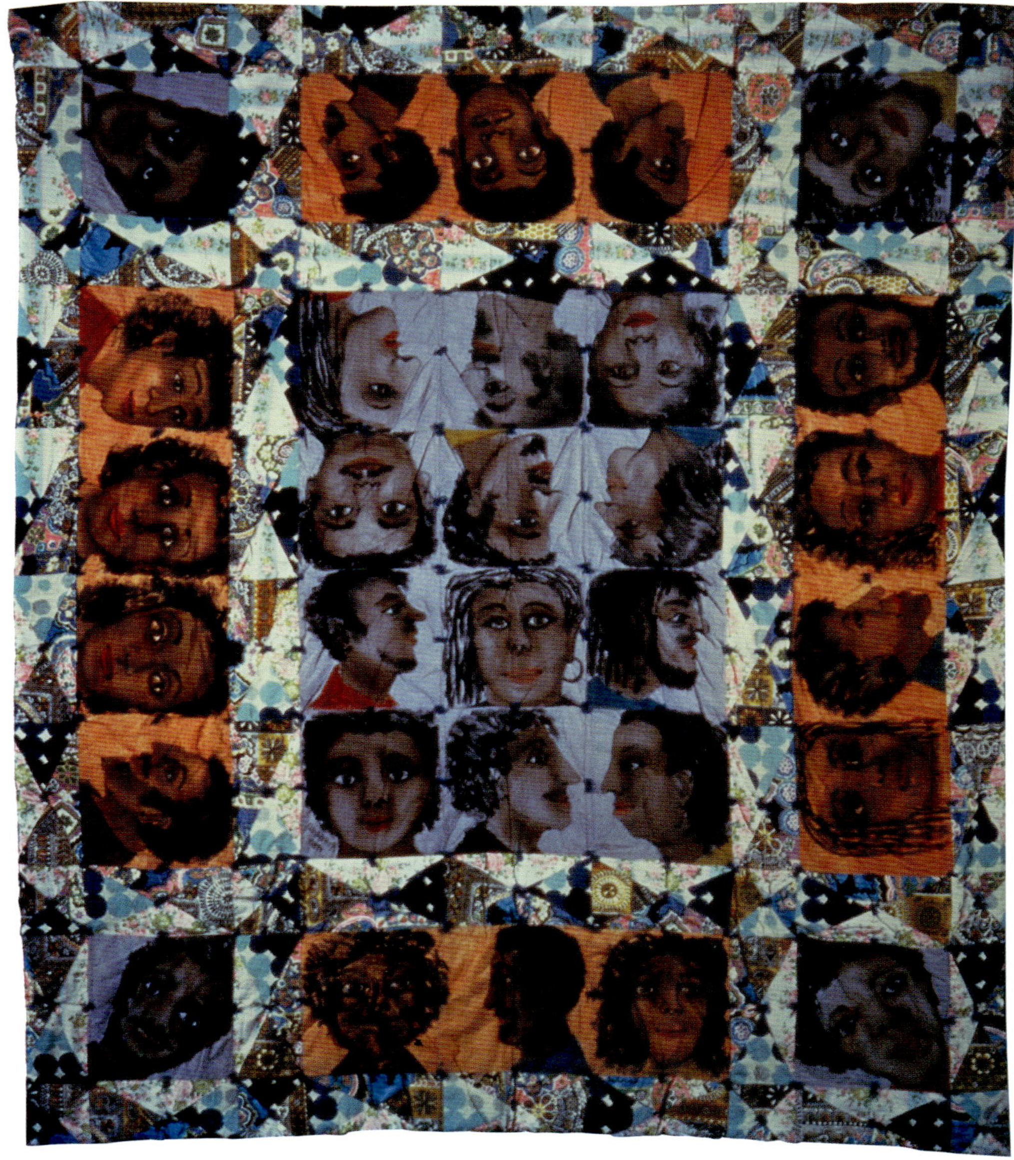

40 Echoes of Harlem, *1980, acrylic on canvas; dyed, painted, and pieced fabric, 96 x 84 in.*

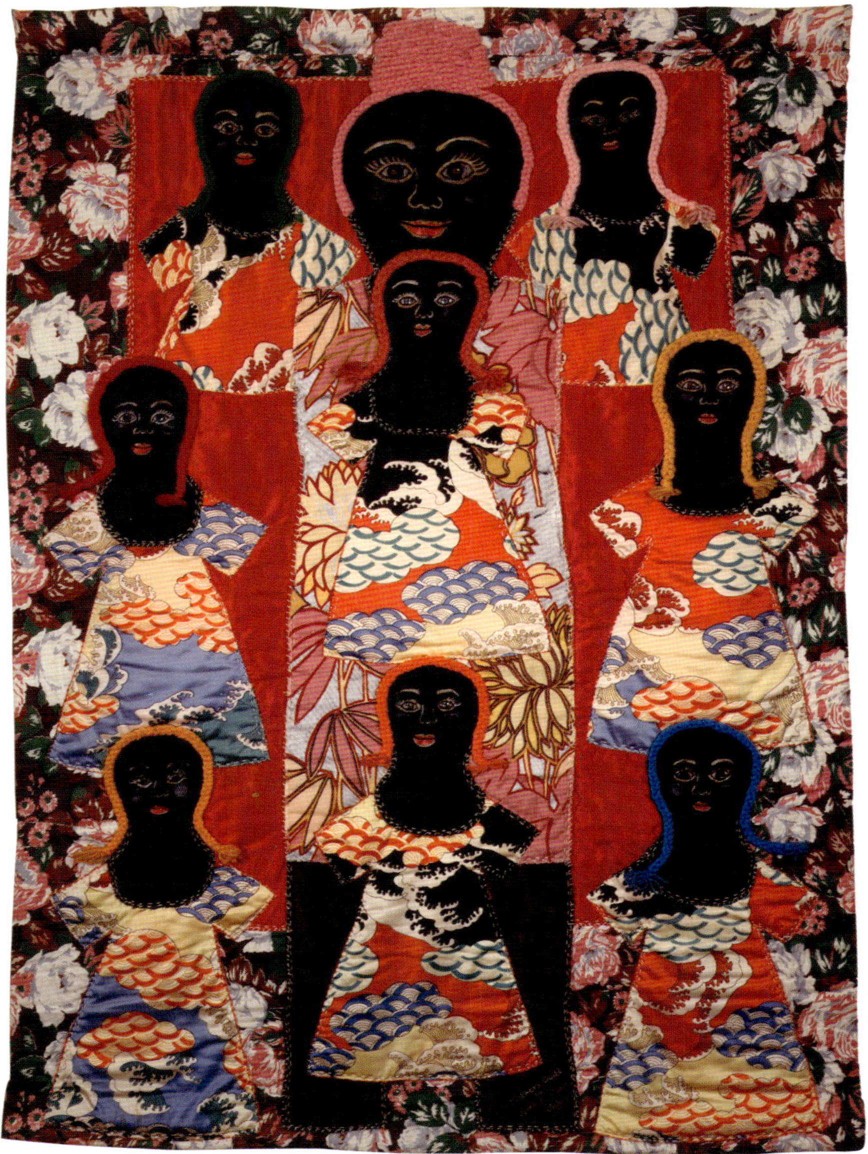

41 Mother's Quilt, *1983, painted, appliquéd, and embroidered fabric with sequins, 58 x 43½ in.*

Faith signed the screenprint version of *Garden Party #1* at her studio on June 18, 2002. This was my first screenprint for Faith, and I wanted to remain faithful to her painterly style, not merely create a reproduction of an already existing work.

She had a number of prints that were of this nature. In some cases they were smaller versions of an original, but some were almost as large as her paintings. As a printmaker I always consider a print that has discernable handwork to be of greater quality than one that is mechanical in its appearance. The silkscreen process was designed for commercial applications and therefore by definition, it is a mechanical process. My method of making the process more authentic, and more akin to the artist's original method, is to add painterly effects by hand and block out sections of the screens as each color is printed. This proved to be effective in this piece because the nuances of the background and details of each individual guest unified the entire composition. This time Faith was pleased with the results.

In 2003, shortly after she had completed her *Flag Series*, I invited Faith to participate in a new project initiated by EPI, The Master Artist Master Printmakers Portfolio. This project involved collaboration among eight master artists, of which Faith would be one, and eight master printmakers. Faith agreed to participate and we decided to include her *Freedom Flag Story #1* as her contribution to the portfolio.

In keeping with the collaborative nature of the project, we invited the printer John Phillips from the

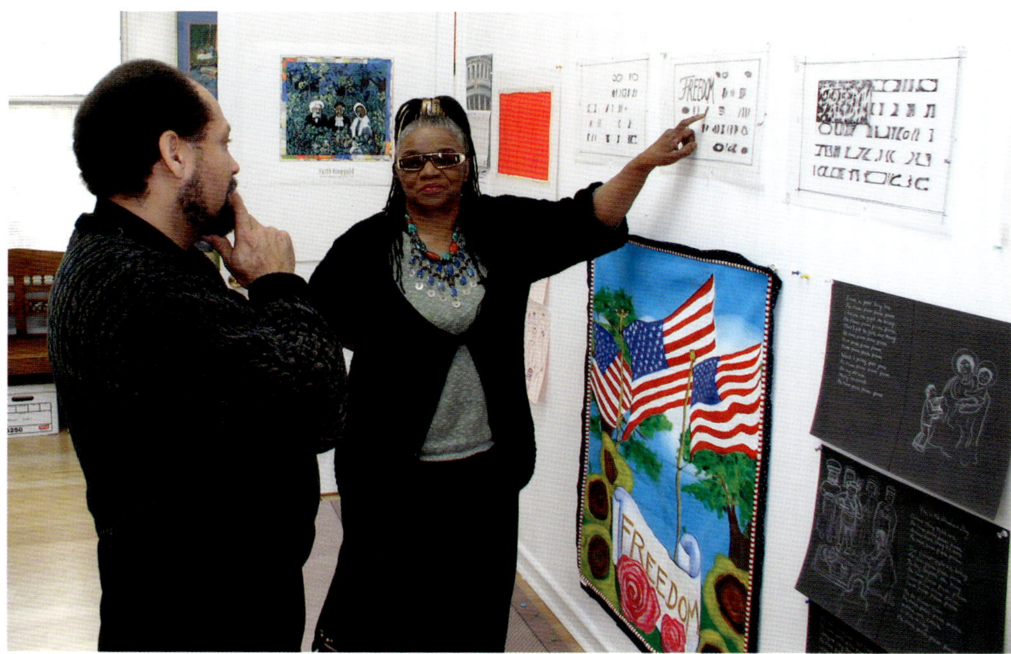

***42** discussion at Faith Ringgold's studio of* Freedom Flag Story #1 *proof, May 2003.*

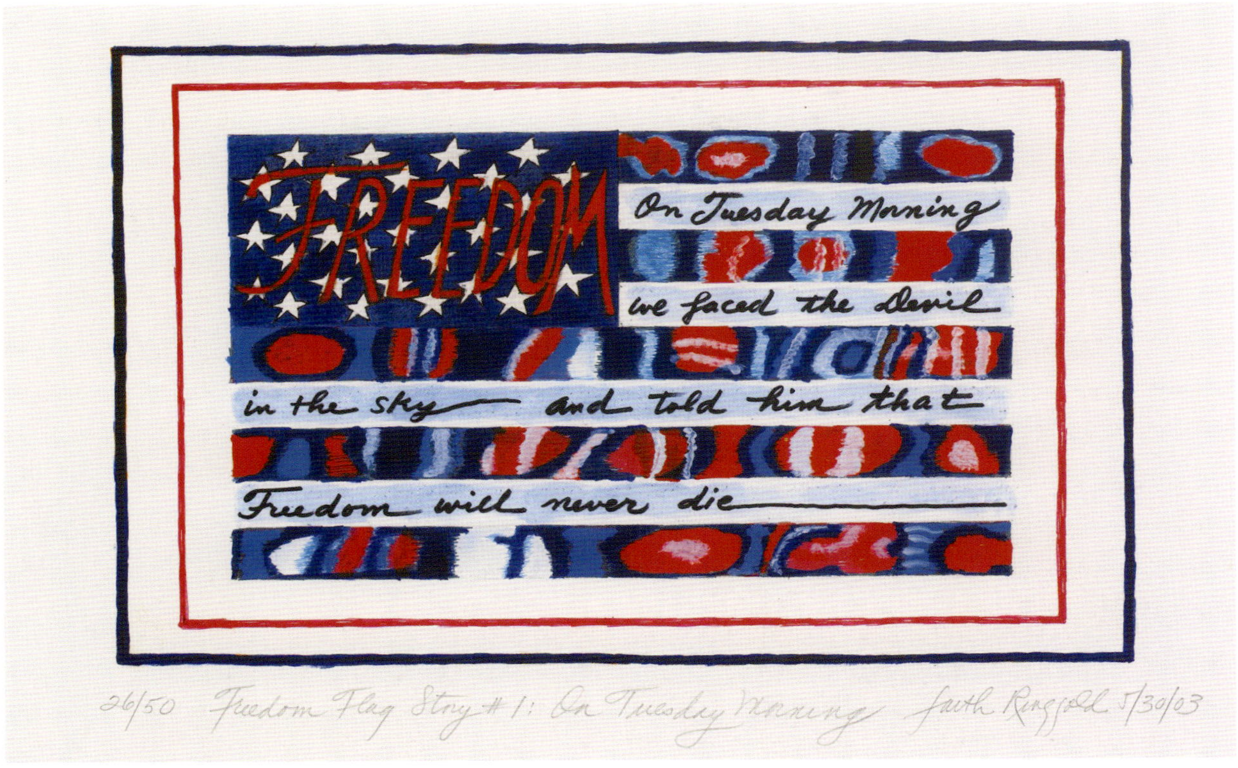

43 Freedom Flag Story #1, *2003, digital print, 15 x 22 in.*

London Printshop in England to participate. The project began as a serigraph print, a process that uses a framed polyester mesh screen that is then processed with a section of the image for each color. The transferring of the image to the screen can be achieved by painstakingly blocking out selected areas by hand or by using photomechanical processes.

During the process each color is proof printed to test the color and fidelity of the images. The initial image was simply not to Faith's liking, and she was quick to say so. She found the interpretation of her colors by our collaborating workshop to be off in their tonality and not up to her standards.

Printmaking is frequently about problem-solving and resolving persistent dilemmas. After a number of additional unacceptable trial prints, we decided to print the edition as a digital print. We used EPI's new large-format digital printer under the guidance of Pat Masters, our digital printing expert. The genesis of this piece was Faith's response to the September 11th attacks in New York City and Washington, D.C.

Artistic Freedom

I have watched freedoms being restricted every day of my life. There are things I know that I am not going to be able to do. At least not right now, not without a fight. Everything becomes a struggle. I don't mind struggling. At least here in America you have the freedom to struggle.

On September 11, 2001, America was stunned as it was attacked from the air by terrorists using our own airplanes. Faith, as an American and native New Yorker, felt violated and forced to respond. She and her assistant, Grace Matthews, collaborated on a hand-painted flag, which hangs from the front door of Faith's home. Faith also began a series of small mixed media flags on paper. Her first in the series was *Freedom Flag Story #1*, on which she wrote *On Tuesday Morning We Faced The Devil in the Sky and Told Him That Freedom Will Never Die.*

We had the opportunity to discuss that somber occasion and how it related to her art:

CURLEE: Is the *Flag Series* indicative of your working style? I mean do you get an idea or an impulse and immediately try to make work from it? Early on in your career you were so prolific I wondered if you were reacting to events around you or to your own research—or were you simply always inspired and continued to produce accordingly?

FAITH: Ah, yes, the *Flag Series* is certainly true to my working style! There was always research. The research was right there on television. I was starting to explain this to myself and how I should feel about it. I asked myself whether these events [of September 11th] were any way similar to the politics of the sixties. I mean should we in any way embrace these people who we know have been persecuted? How should we feel about this, that it has happened on our soil, that it had never happened before? How does this work? This is a complicated situation.

CURLEE: So, you not only processed this as a matter of information for your own self, but for all of us. You seem to feel a deep sense of responsibility to document this event for your fellow man. Does this reveal how you see your role as an artist? How do you see that role?

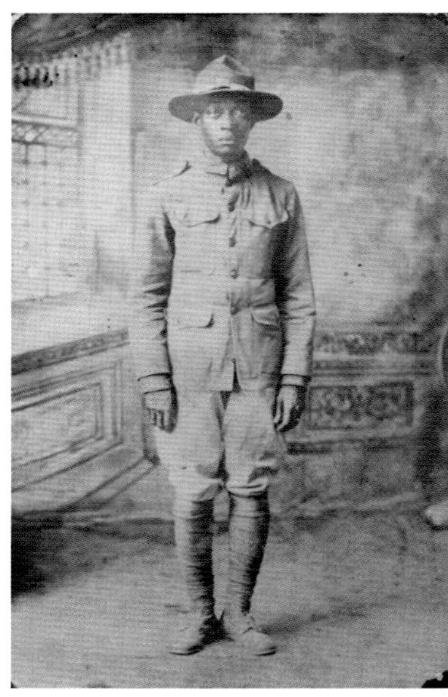

44 Cardoza Posey, Faith's uncle, in World War I soldier's uniform, France, 1918.

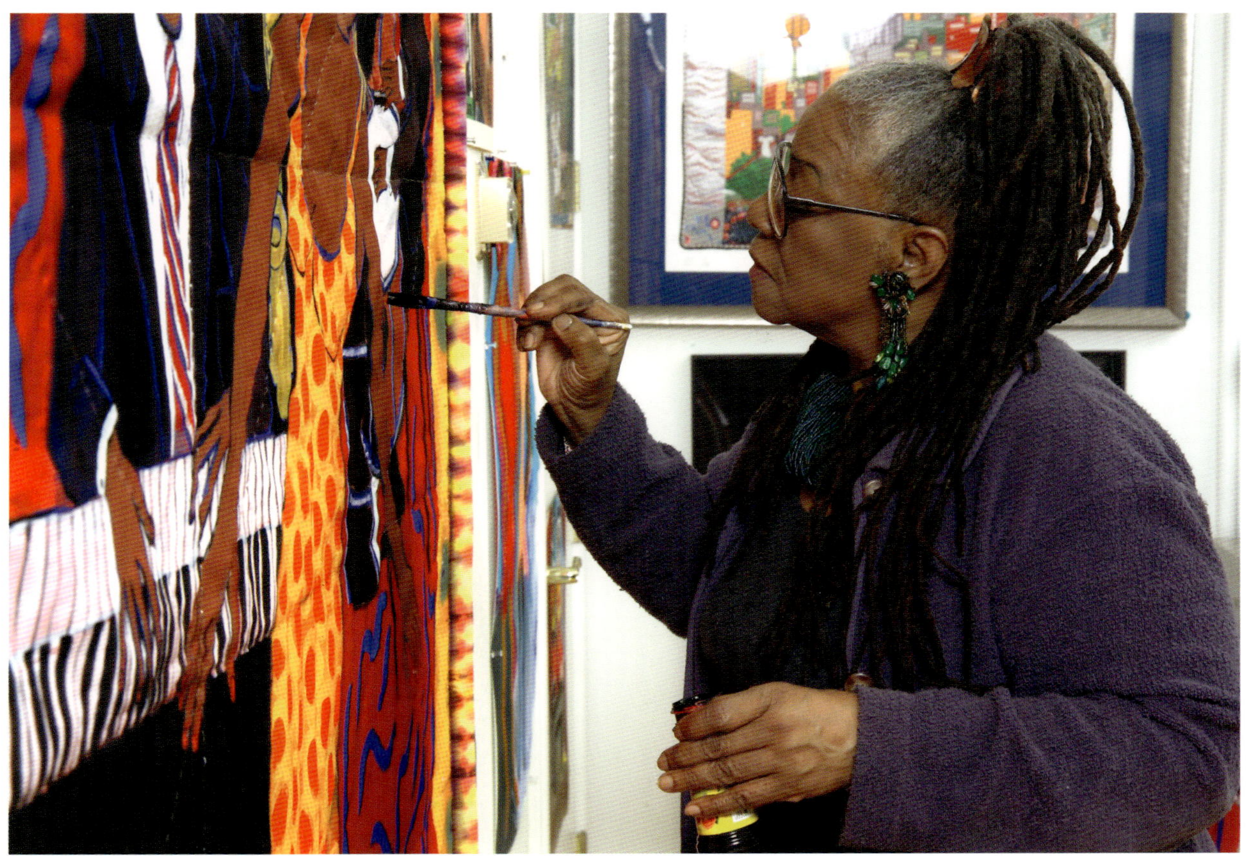

45 Faith Ringgold painting in her studio, July 1, 2004.

FAITH: [I want to] mark this place in our history so that we can comprehend what it would be like to lose the rather fragile freedoms that we do have. You know it is about what those people lost up there in the air. If those people [the terrorists] could have managed to succeed in taking over the country, we would not be in better hands.

Freedom is all the more precious to Faith because she understands that it is not guaranteed. Experiences in her life taught her that our freedoms have to be fought for and protected. As a child she was told of the return of the triumphant black Doughboys from France. Those returning heroes marched down Broadway in full battlefield regalia, representing their valor against the Germans. Faith's uncle, Cardoza Posey, was in the army during WWI and went off to fight in France. He was the pride of the family.

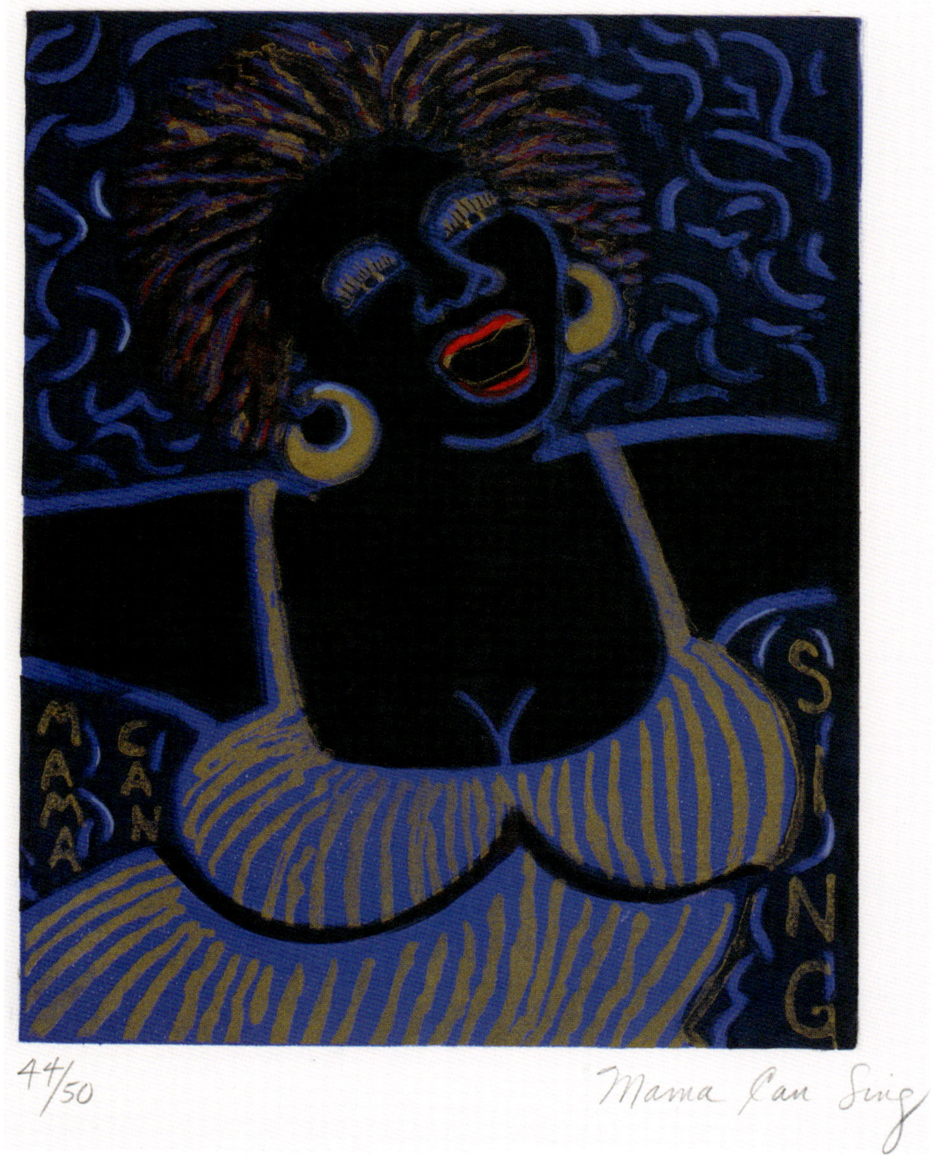

46 Mama Can Sing, *November 21, 2003, color etching, 15 x 22 in.*

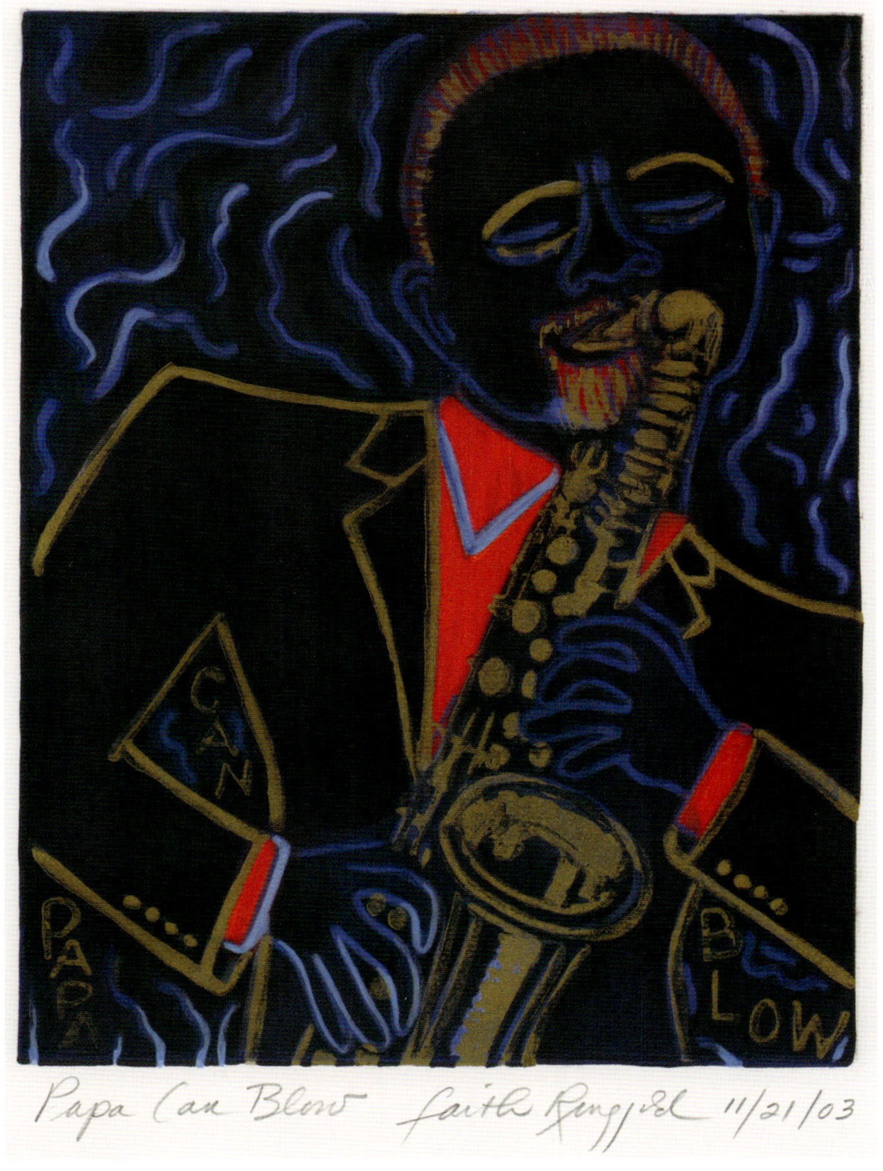

47 Papa Can Blow, *November 21, 2003, color etching, 15 x 22 in.*

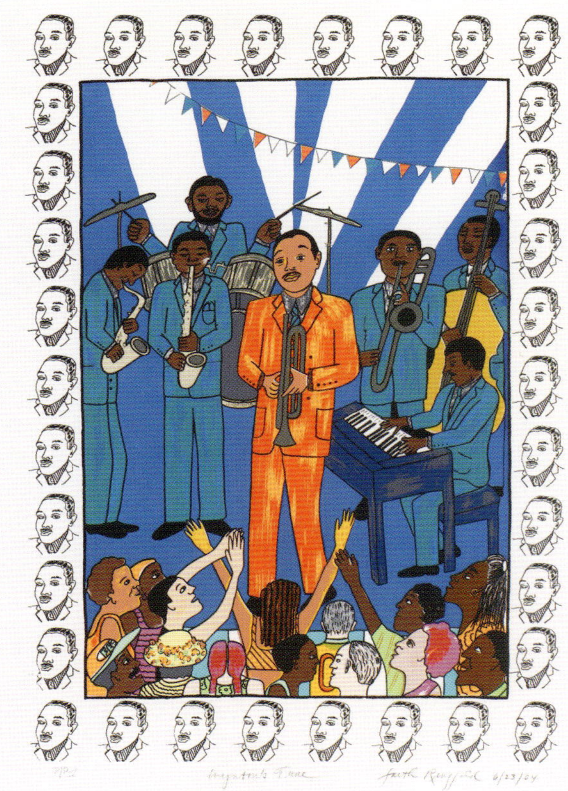

48 Wynton's Tune, *June 23, 2004, serigraph, 22 x 30 in.*

Faith's personal history is also the history of black people and American people. She aimed to express that fully in her new body of work titled the *Jazz Series*, begun in 2002.

Faith has always had a deep appreciation for the creative genius of jazz music and the colorful individuals who performed it. Like the jazz musician, she views herself as a path breaker and has tried to be as innovative and improvisational.

For her, the jazz musician personifies the raw unadulterated experience black people express on an emotional and spiritual level. These musicians play from a place of direct response, a response to a personalizing of a collective experience that is then offered to the listener in a conversational form.

The Jazz Age began in the first decade of the twentieth century, about the same time as the Harlem Renaissance. However, in spite of this cultural and creative eruption of literature, music, and art, many thought this Negro music, with its rhythmic beats and sexually provocative movements, would poison the youth of America and destroy the moral fiber of all who listened.[11] Faith believes this was just one more way to keep black artists out of the mainstream by assigning derogatory meanings to their work.

When I visited Faith's studio in the winter of 2002, I saw the first pieces of this new series up on the wall. Some were rough sketches, while others were at a more advanced stage of development. In all of the works, you could see Faith's signature line giving each figure movement and life. The figures swayed as if they were alive, and if you listened with your eyes, you could hear the music.

When I left her studio that day, I was anxious to get back to Easton. Images of my own were swirling in my head. The two-hour drive was maddening because I wanted to be in the studio with a paintbrush instead of clutching a steering wheel in heavy traffic.

When an artist works closely with someone as prolific as Faith, it is impossible not to feel guilty if the canvas hasn't been touched in a day or so. Her energy was like a palpable force pushing me back to my own work.

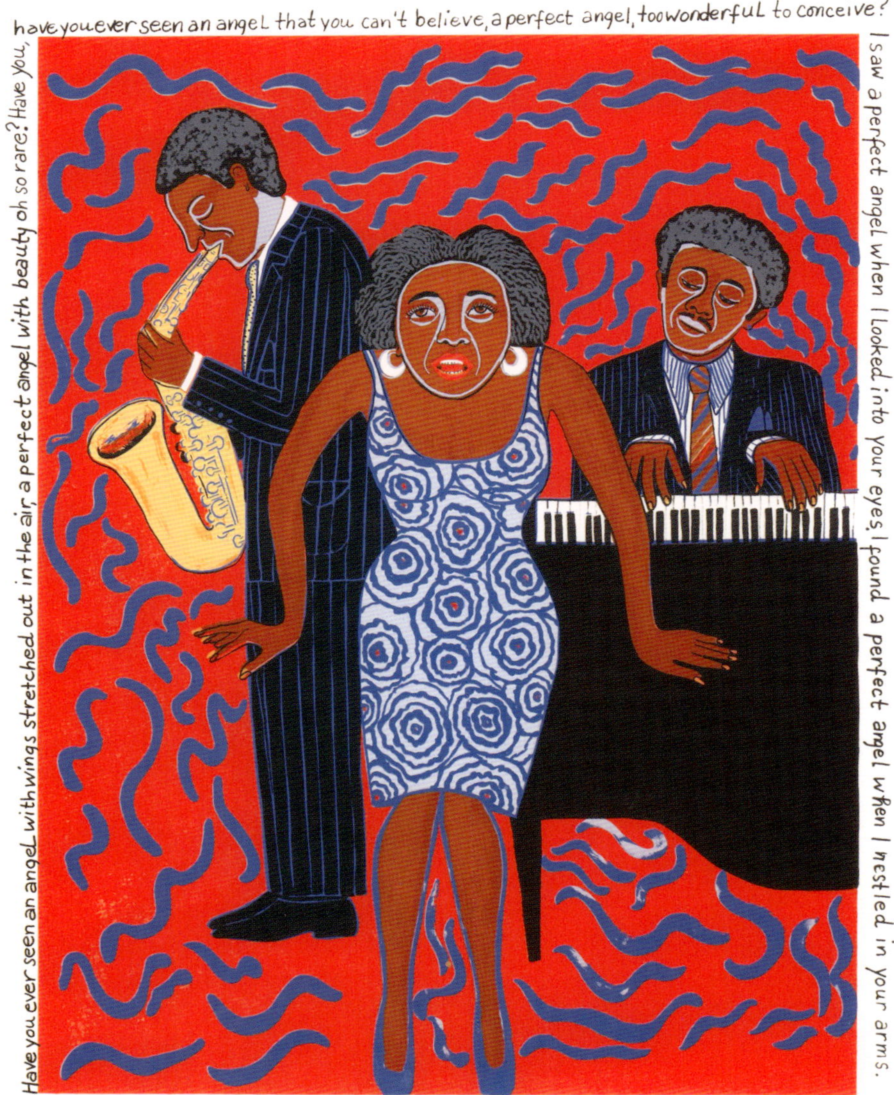

49 Mama Can Sing You Put the Devil in Me: Jazz Series, *July 28, 2004, serigraph, 22 x 30 in.*

Faith showed me two pieces that she had just completed, and she was clearly very excited about the results. One was called *Mama Can Sing*, and it portrayed a close-up of a full-bodied singer painted in bright blue, red, and gold. The figure was painted on a black background, creating a dramatic effect. The second and matching piece was entitled *Papa Can Blow*, which was executed in the same palette. Faith showed me the preliminary drawings for these two pieces, done on black paper, as well as others that she had been working on over the past year.

We agreed to print both pieces as a diptych, and I suggested that we print them as a multi-plate etching to retain the richness of the color. Faith prepared individual drawings for each color. These would be translated into plates that, when bitten in an acid bath, would produce the rich velvety quality that she wanted.

We also decided to deeply etch the final gold plate to produce a relief effect. After resolving all the issues related to the print, I also asked her to consider allowing us to print this new work as a collector's print to benefit EPI and the student-based programming. Smiling, Faith agreed and said she would be happy to support EPI in this way if it would help. Faith can be surprisingly unassuming and self-effacing at times. I knew that it definitely would be an asset to have a Faith Ringgold. This was to become EPI's first collector's print and the piece sold out immediately.

During this period, I would visit Faith often, both in preparation for the Allentown show and to review a number of print projects we had in progress. Two of these print projects were commissions, and one was for the Collectors Guild of the National Black Arts Festival. The latter was a thirteen-color serigraph and depicts one of Faith's favorite jazz musicians, Wynton Marsalis. She entitled the print *Wynton's Tune*. It was unveiled in Atlanta, Georgia, on July 18, 2004. Faith and I both traveled to Atlanta for the event. Faith was one of the featured artists of the festival and presented a lecture to a full house at the High Museum. I mounted an exhibition of works of African American artists from EPI's collection, including works by Faith.

The second commission was for the Allentown Art Museum as a special feature of the upcoming exhibition. The image selected for this print was taken from Faith's new *Jazz Series*, and is one of my personal favorites. It is called *Mama Can Sing You Put The Devil in Me*.

The third print project that I had been working on for the past year was from the *Jones Road Series* and was a collagraph. It uses modeling paste, acrylic paint, and Carborundum grit. The plates were made from these materials to create a painterly effect, providing the texture and consistency that Faith had achieved in her paintings. I also wanted this print to be the largest collagraph printed of Faith's work to date.

In 1997, Faith had a beautiful collagraph printed by Bill Kelly at Brighton Press in California. It hung on her studio wall and every time I passed it, I would remark to her that I could print one larger and better. Faith soon tired of my repeated boast and eventually told me to stop promising and "Just do it." Since then, I have created the plates and pulled five proofs. The process is very laborious because each of the three plates is 36 x 42 inches in size and has to be hand-inked and printed individually. It usually takes up to an hour for each plate to be printed.

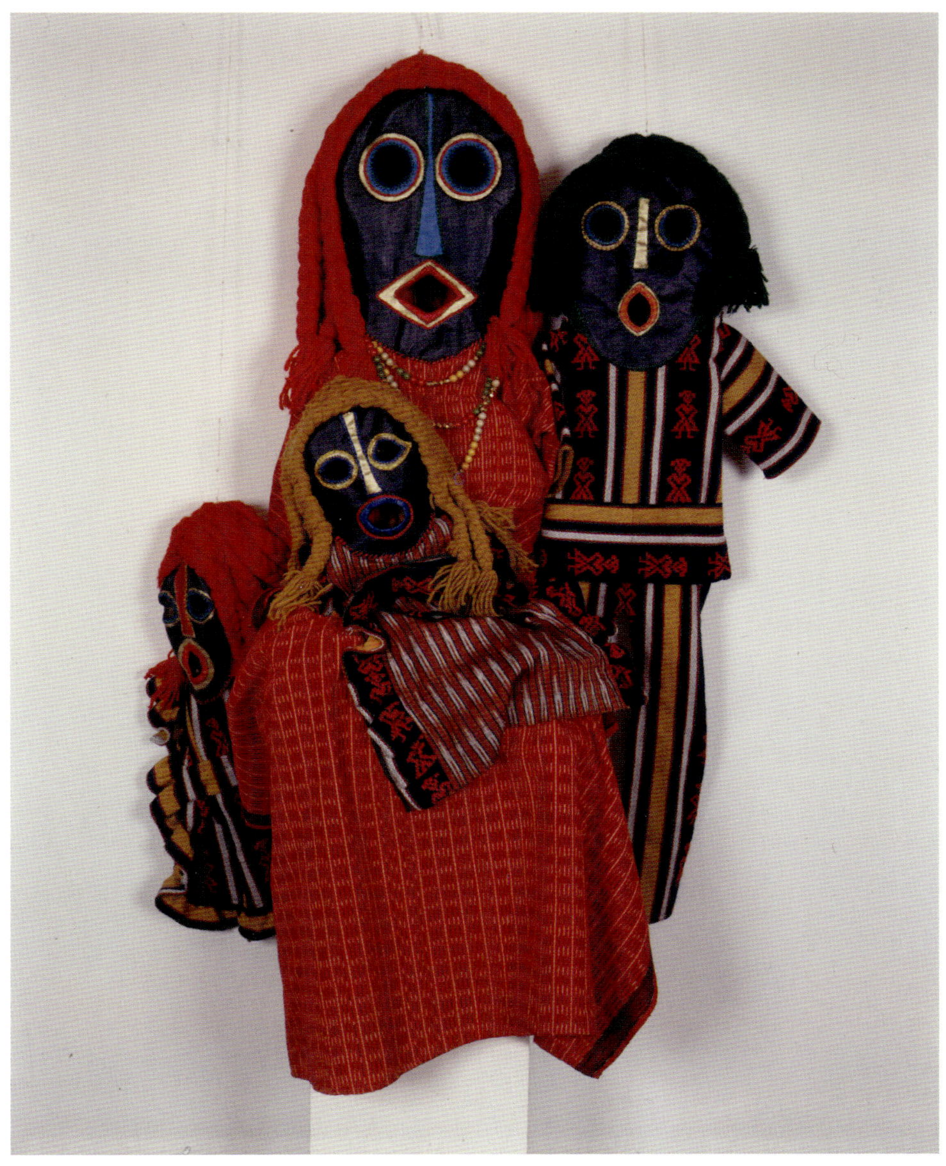

50 Mrs. Jones and Family: The Family of Women Mask Series, *1973, acrylic on canvas; embroidered and pieced fabric, 60 x 12 x 16 in.*

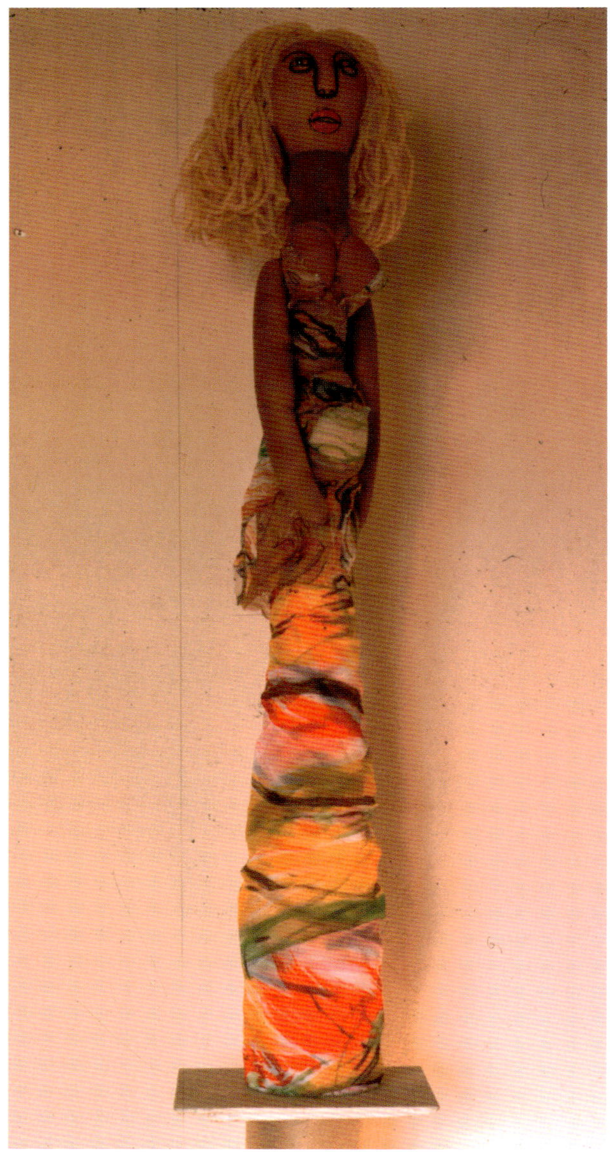

51 Yvonne: Woman on a Pedestal Series, *1979, mixed media soft sculpture.*

In preparation for the show, I also visited Faith's dealers, Dorian and Jeff Bergen at ACA Galleries. During one particular visit, Dorian invited me to view works by Faith that had just been sent back from a traveling exhibition. I saw a number of Faith's works that I had never viewed, including *Mrs. Jones and Family* from her *The Family of Women Mask Series*, 1973, and the soft sculptures, *Chee Chee* from 1978 and *Evelyn* and *Yvonne* from 1979. These reconfirmed for me the broad scope of Faith's subjects and creativity .

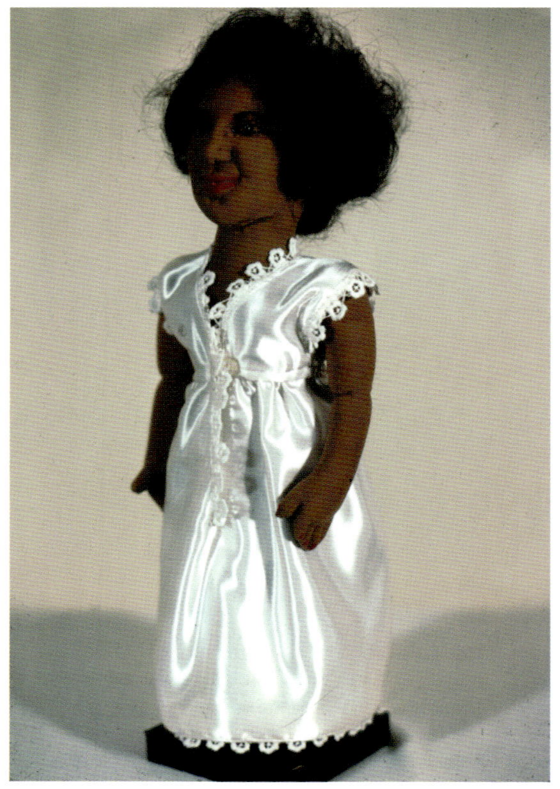

52 Chee Chee: International Doll Series, *1978, mixed media soft sculpture.*

IN THE STUDIO

Faith allows me to move freely through the studio, looking at works I might include in the Allentown show. Many are over twenty years old but look as if she had just made them. I am struck by the *Mourning Mask* of 1989, made of black fabric and hanging above her computer station. One piece becomes more disturbing the longer I look at it. It is a small mixed media sculpture with beaded work on its sides and an interior that is covered in a replica of the American flag. Inside this box lies a flag-covered coffin with a vintage photograph of a young black soldier from World War I, an original KKK pendant attached to the flag just above his head. The piece is titled *Bubba Lost His Life* and was made in 1989. Every time I look at this piece I am transported back to my own days in the army, sweating in the heat of Texas during basic training and wondering why and when I would be sent to Vietnam.

On a blustery winter day in December of 2003, I returned to the studio to pick up the signed print *Mama Can Sing* and *Papa Can Blow* and to introduce Faith to the executive director of the Allentown Art Museum, David Brigham, and to the museum's textile curator, Ruth Saliklis. We found that Faith had completed a new book *O Holy Night* and was busily reviewing the final pages for the printer.

Faith was excited to learn that the original illustrations from *O Holy Night* would be exhibited at the Metropolitan Museum of Art at Christmastime, and there would be related events—a book signing by her and a performance of Christmas carols by the Boys Choir of Harlem.

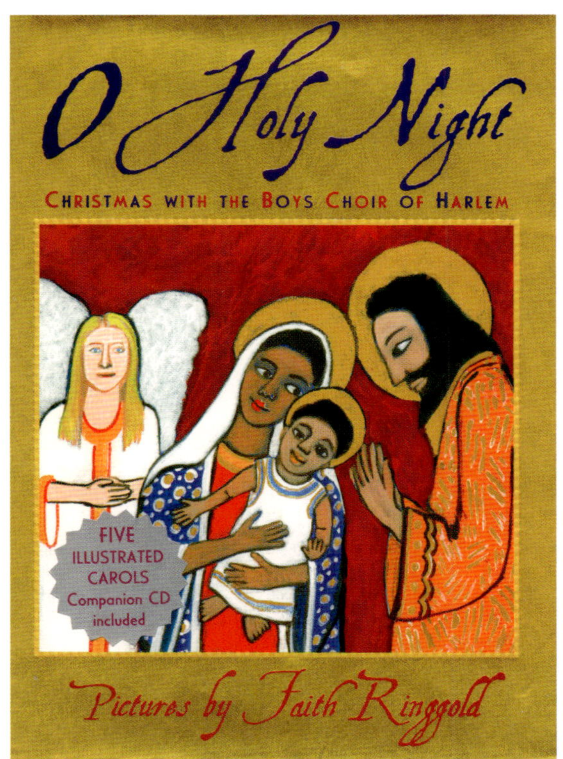

53 O Holy Night, *2004.*

Faith explained that the Metropolitan had purchased *Freedom of Speech Flag* in 2000 and showed it for the first time in 2003. They also bought the rights to produce a poster from it as well. It has become a Met bestseller and is included in their 2004 *Timeline of Art History* Series.

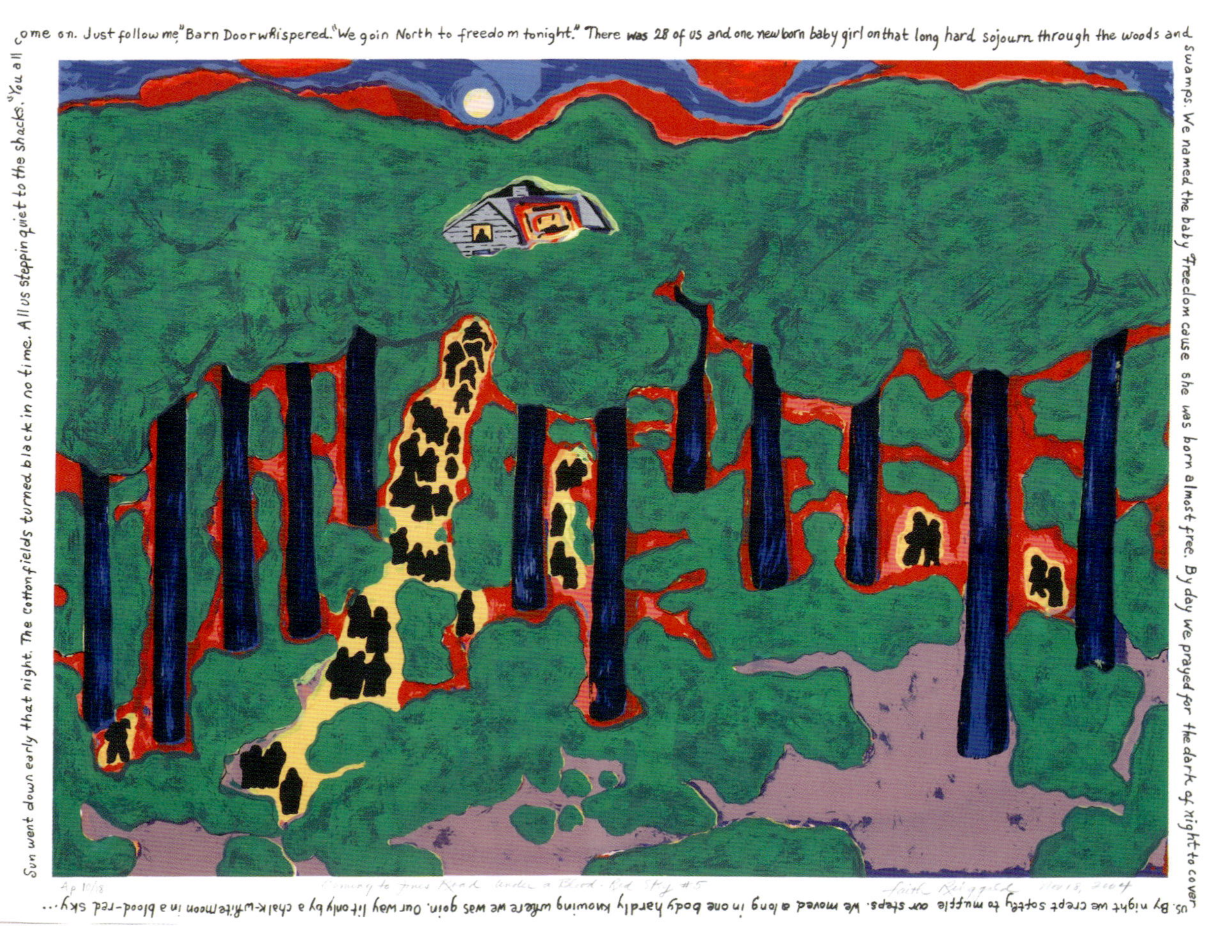

54 Coming To Jones Road Series: Under a Blood-Red Sky #5, *2004, serigraph, 35 x 45 in.*

Soon after our departure, Faith called me with more thrilling news. She explained that the Metropolitan Museum of Art wanted to commission her to create a print for their Mezzanine Gallery. She asked me would I like to make the print. I said I would be honored. We decided to do something from the *Jones Road Series* and to make it big. We would produce a large serigraphy with dramatic colors and text on the border.

Faith stands looking out of her studio window at her home on Jones Road in Englewood, New Jersey. She imagines the journey that her ancestors made during the dark of night with all their belongings tied up in a sack as they escaped to freedom. Most, if not all, are barefoot and full of apprehension as they watch the window lights for a sign that they have found a place of refuge from their long trek from slavery. Some are young and some are old. There are children and babies clutched tightly in their mothers' exhausted arms. Faith imagines their hunger. She imagines their shivering bodies huddled together to protect themselves from the bitter cold, and yet they are still moving in fear of being caught by bounty hunters.

Coming to Jones Road #4, entitled *Under a Blood Red Sky*, is a visual account of the struggle and the anger that has provided an inner force for Faith, just as it did for the black ancestors who came before her. This is a carefully orchestrated series of paintings and prints about the Underground Railroad. Metaphorically, it suggests that the journey is not yet over and that the freedom won is a veiled and amorphous prize. Faith uses the color red prominently in all of these works. The color is symbolic of fierce passion for freedom and a rebellious spirit.

It is a spirit Faith knows well. As we wrapped up plans for the Allentown show, Faith told me about her move to Englewood, New Jersey.

"I moved here in 1992 and decided that I was going to make a studio over my house. The house was bought and it was mine and I thought that it would be great with a studio on top.

"There is a [zoning] board that you have to go to and get it approved. I went, and immediately hostile neighbors surrounded me.

"At a particularly tense moment one man got up and said that he paid a healthy tax and that it was a beautiful neighborhood and the community had a wonderful quality of life and that it was all going to change if my studio was built.

"And I am... I am amazed! I mean I had thought that I had been subjected to some racism in my life, but I had never been subjected to anything like this before.

"Unfortunately, the message was clear. It's going be black folks coming in and out. The quality of life that guy described would be lost. Now this is what I had to put up with!

"So I said, they don't like me? Well I'm going to bring all my ancestors in the *Coming to Jones Road Series*. It made me realize what they must have gone through because they were so much less powerful than I am, you know? I knew that I could get around these people, but I still had to be subjected to this crap. See what they make you do is, they make you spend money and they hold you up. They make you waste time and money, for your freedom. And that's what I had to do. It took about six years to get the studio built.

"So that's the story of *Coming to Jones Road*.

"It's an ancestral story, a story that most of us haven't got much of a link to. Except, that most neighborhoods in America are racially divided—black people live here, white people live there. That's known. I'd always lived in Harlem. I'd never had any problem with that. And that was good enough for me. I've lived in Harlem all my life, and I didn't necessarily know my neighbors, but they were all right. Whoever they were was okay with me. It was a community that was very homogeneous. However, if I had known that these people in Englewood were going to attack me the way they did—without even knowing me, people who lived right around me—I would not have bought this house. But once we bought the house, I could not allow them to deprive me of my freedom to build my studio. To do otherwise would be giving up my right to liberty and my right to the pursuit of happiness. This house... I love this house. I love my garden. I love everything about it. I've learned to ignore these people. I've always had racist people around me. "

As Faith told me her story I asked her, "When you look out your studio window, what do you see?"

"I see my determination to be free in America. And I'd like to pass that on, because I know that a lot of people have had the problems I have. And a lot of people have had to give up because they couldn't afford to persevere. You see they couldn't afford to win! And freedom is not free. You've got to pay for that dream. And I was determined that I was not going to let them win, but if I had known in advance that I was the one that was integrating this community, I would not have been interested. I've never been interested in integrating something. "

So, I said to Faith, "When you stand and look out that window you see those who couldn't stand in this room and look out this window and look at that garden?"

"That's right. Those people, my people, if they had not persevered, I would not be here. It was a little thing for me to do, but it was a big thing for them. It was huge for them, you know. But, yes that was what *Coming to Jones Road* is about. And for the *Jazz Series* I borrowed the story of our ancestors when they were down and out and singing the blues. A beautiful art form came out from all of that misery and suffering. So I said, let me turn this into something beautiful. This doesn't have to be something ugly. This can be something beautiful. "

"I can beautify this. I will beautify this!'

"The black musicians took all the pain and suffering and turned it into music. This is characteristic of what we do as black people. We had to do that."

"It's what I've done with my work. So it just fits me perfectly, you know? And you gain such strength from them. Because their music just identifies this country. When you listen to their music you not only think black, you think America. You think American. Those musicians don't have to say that they are black. We all know who they are."

"When I was in elementary school I used to see reproductions of Horace Pippin's 1942 painting called *John Brown Going to His Hanging* in my text books. I didn't know Pippin was a black person. No one ever told me that. I was much, much older before I found out that there was at least one black artist in my history books. Only one. Now that didn't help me. That wasn't good enough for me. How come I didn't have that source of power? It is important. That's why I am a black artist. It is exactly why I say who I am."

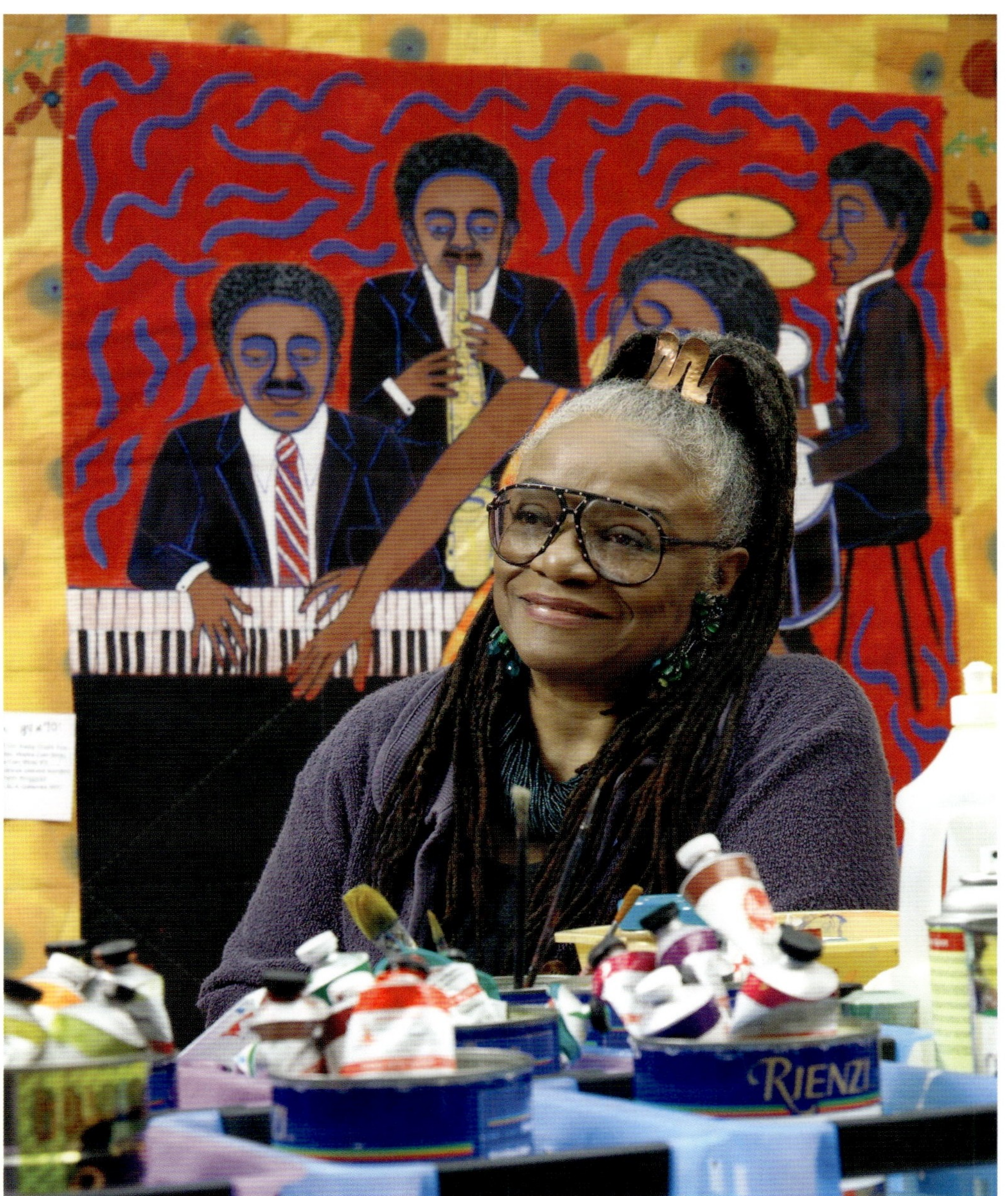
RIENZI

Endnotes

Unless noted below, all quotes by Faith Ringgold are taken from the author's interviews with the artist between 2001 and 2004.

1. Faith Ringgold, *We Flew over the Bridge* (Boston: Bulfinch Press, 1995) 9.
2. Ringgold, *We Flew over the Bridge*, 8.
3. Albert Murray, *Stomping the Blues* (New York: DaCapo Press, 1989).
4. Lisa E. Farrington, *Faith Ringgold* (San Francisco: Pomegranate Communications, Inc., 2004) 75.
5. Ringgold, *We Flew over the Bridge*, 159-60.
6. Faith Ringgold. Lecture at the High Museum. Atlanta, Georgia. July 18, 2004.
7. Ringgold, *We Flew over the Bridge*, 166-69.
8. Ringgold, *We Flew over the Bridge*, 191.
9. Ringgold, *We Flew over the Bridge*, 193.
10. Ringgold, *We Flew over the Bridge*, 197.
11. Geoffrey C. Ward and Ken Burns. *Jazz: A History of America's Music* (New York: Alfred A. Knopf, 2000) 11.

Picture Credits

Front cover: Hub Willson Photography.
Back cover and flaps: © Faith Ringgold, Collection of the Artist, courtesy ACA Galleries, New York.
Endpapers: © Faith Ringgold (1) Collection of the Harold Washington Library, Chicago, Illinois. (2) Collection of Francie Bishop Goode. (3) Collection of the Worcester Art Museum, Worcester, Massachusetts. (4) Collection of John Spohler.
Title page: Hub Willson Photography.
1: © Faith Ringgold, printed by EPI, photograph by Robert Walch, Collection of the Allentown Art Museum, Allentown, Pennsylvania.
2: Hub Willson Photography.
3: © Faith Ringgold, Collection of the Artist, courtesy ACA Galleries, New York.
4: © Faith Ringgold, Collection of the Artist, courtesy ACA Galleries, New York.
5: © Faith Ringgold, Collection of the Artist, courtesy ACA Galleries, New York.
6: © Faith Ringgold, Collection of the Artist, courtesy ACA Galleries, New York.
7: © Faith Ringgold, Collection of the Artist, courtesy ACA Galleries, New York.
8: © Faith Ringgold, Collection of Francie Bishop Goode.
9: © Faith Ringgold, Collection of the Worcester Art Museum, Worcester, Massachusetts.
10: © Faith Ringgold, Collection of the St. Louis Art Museum, St. Louis, Missouri.
11: EPI Archives.
12: © Faith Ringgold printed by EPI, photograph by Robert Walch.
13: © Faith Ringgold, Collection of the High Museum of Art, Atlanta, Georgia.
14: © Faith Ringgold, Collection of the Harold Washington Library, Chicago, Illinois.
15: © Faith Ringgold, Collection of John Spohler.
16: © Faith Ringgold, Collection of The Studio Museum, Harlem.
17: © Faith Ringgold, Collection of the Solomon R. Guggenheim Museum, New York.
18: Faith Ringgold Archives.
19: Faith Ringgold Archives.
20: Faith Ringgold Archives.
21: photograph by George Panichas.
22: photograph by Ananda Holton.
23: © Faith Ringgold, Collection of the Artist, courtesy ACA Galleries, New York.
24: © Faith Ringgold, Collection of the Sandor Family.
25: © Faith Ringgold, Collection of the Philadelphia Museum of Art, Philadelphia, Pennsylvania.
26: © Faith Ringgold, printed by EPI, photograph by Robert Walch.
27: © Faith Ringgold, Collection of Linda Lee Alter, Philadelphia, Pennsylvania.
28: © Faith Ringgold, printed by EPI, photograph by Robert Walch.
29: photograph by George Panichas.
30: EPI Archives.
31: Faith Ringgold Archives.
32: EPI Archives.
33: © Faith Ringgold, printed by EPI, photograph by Robert Walch.
34: © Faith Ringgold, Collection of the Artist, courtesy ACA Galleries, New York.
35: © Faith Ringgold, Collection of the Artist, courtesy ACA Galleries, New York.
36: © Faith Ringgold, Collection of the Artist, courtesy ACA Galleries, New York.
37: photograph by Nat Hentaff.
38: Faith Ringgold Archives.
39: Faith Ringgold Archives.
40: © Faith Ringgold, Collection of Philip Morris Companies, Inc.
41: © Faith Ringgold, Collection of Ed Bradley.
42: EPI Archives.
43: © Faith Ringgold, printed by EPI, photograph by Robert Walch.
44: Faith Ringgold Archives.
45: Hub Willson Photography.
46: © Faith Ringgold, printed by EPI, photograph by Robert Walch.
47: © Faith Ringgold, printed by EPI, photograph by Robert Walch.
48: © Faith Ringgold, printed by EPI, photograph by Robert Walch.
49: © Faith Ringgold, printed by EPI, photograph by Robert Walch, Collection of the Allentown Art Museum, Allentown, Pennsylvania.
50: © Faith Ringgold, Collection of the Artist, courtesy ACA Galleries, New York.
51: © Faith Ringgold, Private Collection.
52: © Faith Ringgold, Private Collection.
53: © Faith Ringgold, cover of *O Holy Night*, published by Harper Collins, 2004, photograph by Robert Walch.
54: © Faith Ringgold, printed by EPI, photograph by Robert Walch, Courtesy Metropolitan Museum of Art, Mezzanine Gallery.
Page 63: Hub Willson Photography.

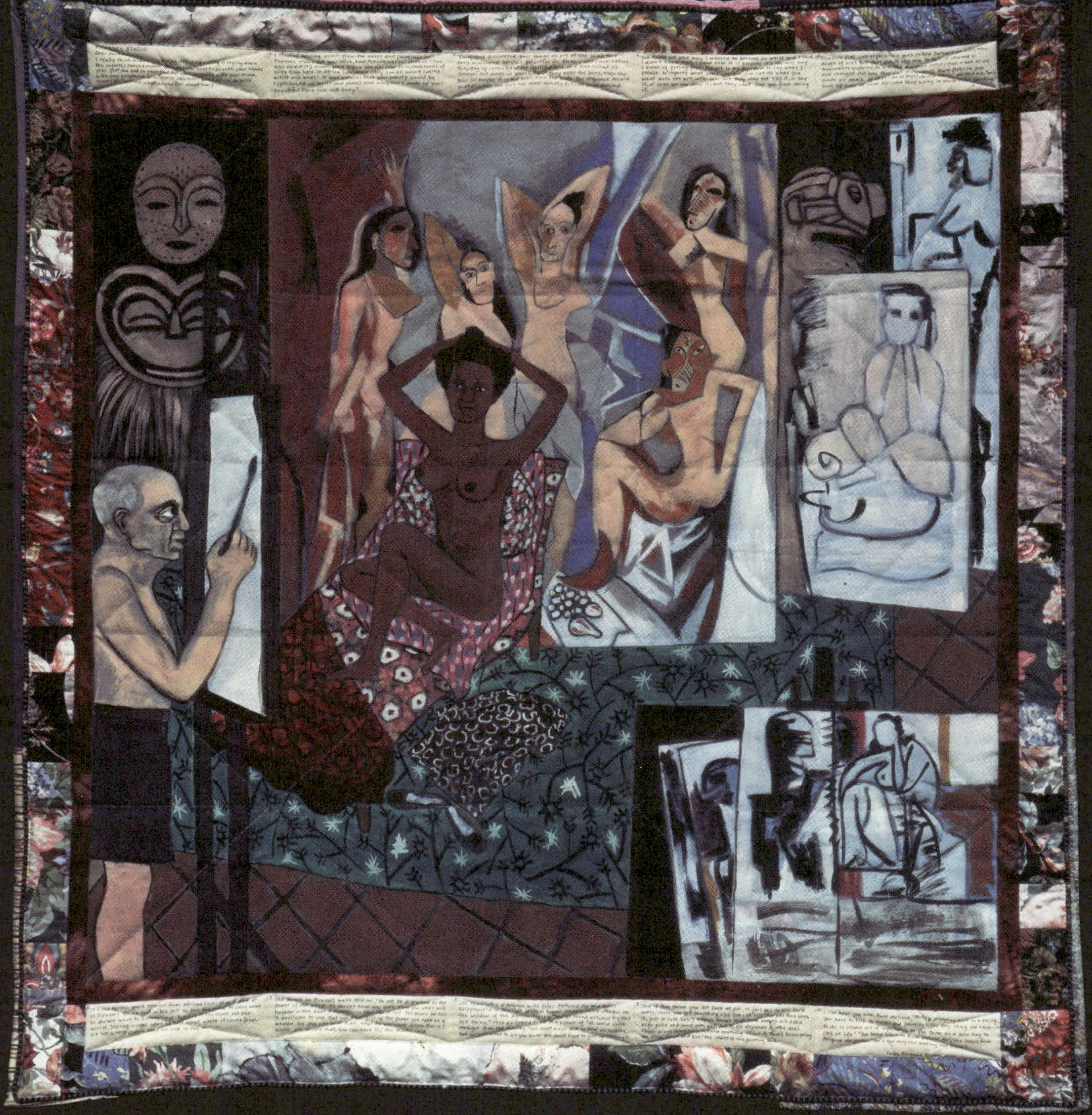